GCSE
ICT
The Revision Guide

This book is for anyone doing **GCSE ICT** (Information and Communication Technology).

Whatever subject you're doing it's the same old story — there are lots of facts and you've just got to learn them. This one is no different.

Happily this CGP book gives you all that important information as clearly and concisely as possible.

It's also got some daft bits in to try and make the whole experience at least vaguely entertaining for you.

<u>What CGP is all about</u>

Our sole aim here at CGP is to produce the highest quality books — carefully written, immaculately presented and dangerously close to being funny.

Then we work our socks off to get them out to you — at the cheapest possible prices.

Contents

SECTION SIX — MEASUREMENT AND CONTROL

SECTION SEVEN — NETWORKS AND COMMUNICATION

SECTION EIGHT — MAKING ICT SYSTEMS

SECTION NINE — PROCESSING INFORMATION

SECTION TEN — OTHER ICT ISSUES

Published by CGP

Editors:
Murray Hamilton and Andy Park.

Contributors:
Colin Harber Stuart, Charley Darbishire, Simon Little and Glenn Rogers.

Proofreading:
Cassandra Mettleton and Neil Hastings.

With thanks to Jan Greenway for the copyright research.

ISBN: 978 1 84762 172 6

Groovy website: www.cgpbooks.co.uk
Jolly bits of clipart from CorelDRAW®
Printed by Elanders Ltd, Newcastle upon Tyne.

Based on the classic CGP style created by Richard Parsons.

Computers

ICT... <u>Information and Communication Technology</u>. Or as I like to call it... Computers and stuff.

Microprocessors Made the Digital Age Possible

1) <u>Microprocessors</u> (microchips) are in every computer in the world — they're basically the brains of a computer, where all the <u>data</u> is <u>processed</u>.

2) In a computer they're responsible for <u>running computer programs</u>, <u>responding to user input</u> and pretty much <u>everything else</u> that makes a computer what it is.

3) A computer's main <u>processor</u> is the <u>CPU</u> (<u>central processing unit</u>).

4) Microprocessors are installed on <u>circuit boards</u>, along with a load of other <u>chips</u>, <u>wiring</u> and <u>electronic components</u>.

A typical circuit board.

Computers Contain a CPU... Plus Various Other Things

You can't see all the bits listed below in the picture... but they're all in there somewhere.

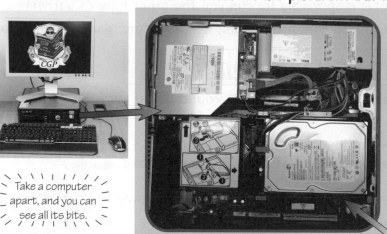

Take a computer apart, and you can see all its bits.

VIDEO CARD
A circuit board that generates <u>video output</u>.

SOUND CARD
Deals with the <u>input</u> and <u>output</u> of <u>sound</u>.

WIRELESS CARD
A device that picks up <u>wireless signals</u>.

MOTHERBOARD
The <u>main circuit board</u> of a computer. It holds the <u>CPU</u>, the <u>memory chips</u>, and various <u>connections</u>.

INTERNAL MEMORY   ROM and RAM (p9).

BACKING STORAGE   the <u>hard drive</u> (p10-11).

There are Computers... and Computers

Computers don't always look like the above pics. Computers can range in size from the <u>mainframes</u> used by businesses (about the size of a <u>small house</u>) to the tiny processors inside your <u>phone</u>.

1) Companies doing a lot of <u>processing</u> (e.g. <u>banks</u>, <u>search engine</u> firms and <u>e-commerce</u> firms on the Internet) need a lot of computing power. They use either <u>mainframes</u> or <u>servers</u>.

2) <u>Mainframes</u> were first developed in the 1960s — they're big and <u>reliable</u>, and often contain <u>multiple</u> copies of each of their parts, so if one fails then they can just switch to another.

3) <u>Servers</u> are fast PCs <u>without</u> most of the bits that normally let you talk to the computer, such as <u>keyboards</u> and <u>screens</u>. Servers can be connected together so they act like a <u>single machine</u> — making it easy to <u>increase</u> or <u>decrease</u> the amount of <u>processing power</u> available by just adding or removing servers. It also means that it usually doesn't matter if any individual machine <u>fails</u>.

4) You wouldn't necessarily know a lot of computers even exist. <u>Embedded</u> computers are inside everyday objects such as washing machines, TVs, central heating systems, cars, phones, watches...

5) And <u>supercomputers</u> are at the <u>cutting edge</u> of computer technology. They contain the fastest, most powerful processors that computer manufacturers can make.

Mainframe — the one that decides a game of snooker...

Some people say they <u>don't</u> own a computer. I mostly don't believe them, since microprocessors and computers are inside <u>so many</u> things these days. Make sure you know all this stuff.

Computers

Computers are basically collections of various bits of <u>hardware</u> and <u>software</u>.
This is probably going to be an easy page, but make sure you know all the stuff <u>properly</u>.

Hardware Means Equipment You Can Touch...

1) The term "<u>hardware</u>" refers to all the parts of a computer system you can <u>physically touch</u>.
So a <u>keyboard</u> is a piece of hardware. As is a <u>mouse</u>. And a <u>monitor</u>.

2) A <u>hard drive</u> is hardware too. It's not as easy to touch as a mouse — you'd probably need to
take your computer apart first. But if you did that, you <u>could</u> touch it, so it's hardware.

...Software Means Programs

<u>Software</u> means the <u>programs</u> that a computer runs — they're sets of <u>instructions</u> that get all
the different bits of hardware to work together. Computers use two kinds of software...

1) An <u>operating system</u> (<u>OS</u>) — this is the software that <u>controls</u> the whole computer system, e.g.
Windows®, UNIX®, Mac OS® X. The OS is responsible for running the other type of software...

2) <u>Application Software</u> — this means things like word processors, spreadsheets, games, and so on.

Laptops and Netbooks are Portable Computers

Computers <u>all</u> used to be hefty things that you could only move around if you owned a <u>forklift</u>.
Those days are gone...

LAPTOPS (or NOTEBOOKS) are pretty small — not much bigger than <u>this book</u>
(but usually slightly <u>thicker</u>). They're very <u>portable</u> — they'll fit in a small bag.

NETBOOKS are smaller, like the size of a piece of kitchen towel
(but slightly <u>thicker...</u>). They're very very <u>portable</u>.

Handheld Devices include Tablets and Smartphones

The first handheld devices were called "<u>palmtops</u>" or <u>PDAs</u> (personal digital assistants).
They had basic versions of the software of bigger computers, like word-processors, spreadsheets
and digital organisers. Today's handheld devices are called <u>tablets</u> and <u>smartphones</u>.

- A typical tablet would be <u>slightly smaller</u> than a netbook, but <u>bigger</u> than a mobile phone.
- Tablets have their own <u>operating system</u> and can have various <u>applications</u> loaded onto them.
- They're mainly designed for Internet use, and will have <u>powerful processors</u> and relatively large
<u>high resolution screens</u> for streaming music, video, etc.
- They'll have <u>touch screens</u> (that can be used as a QWERTY keyboard) and probably lots of
other features like <u>personal organiser</u>, <u>navigation</u> system, <u>camera</u>, <u>media players</u>... and so on.
- <u>E-book readers</u> are more basic tablets designed specifically for <u>storing and reading books</u> —
they use a different display technology that is <u>non-reflective</u> and mimics the appearance of real
ink on paper. They have relatively long battery life and are lighter than other tablets.
- <u>Smartphones</u> have many of the same features as tablets (in addition to being mobile phones),
but are considerably smaller and lighter.

Everything's getting smaller and smaller...

Things change pretty fast. No doubt by the time you read this, a typical computer will be about
the size of a <u>fingernail</u>. But the stuff above is what might come up in your <u>exam</u>, so learn it well.

Input Devices

An input device is any <u>hardware</u> which is used to <u>enter data</u> into the computer system.

QWERTY Keyboards are the Most Common Input Device

1) QWERTY keyboards are the most common type of keyboard. The name comes from the <u>first row of letters</u> on the keyboard.

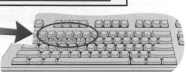

2) Each key is connected to a <u>switch</u> which closes when the key is pressed. This sends a <u>signal</u> to the CPU based on the key's location.

3) QWERTY keyboards are based on the way <u>typewriters</u> were designed.

4) A problem is that keying in can be slow unless the user has been <u>trained</u> or knows how to type.

Concept Keyboards are Faster but More Limited

1) Concept keyboards are typically found in <u>shops</u> and <u>restaurants</u>. Each switch has a <u>symbol</u> (or word) on it, representing a piece of data (e.g. the <u>price</u>) stored in the computer.

2) For example, if you go to a fast-food restaurant and order a bacon-double-turnip burger, the assistant will press the <u>picture</u> of that burger. The CPU then tells a <u>display panel</u> to show the correct price and sends a message to the kitchen and stock-control system.

Concept keyboards are <u>great</u> if you want to key in <u>similar information over and over</u> again.

Mice and the like...

Most people find using a mouse <u>easy</u>. A mouse has <u>two main parts</u>:

1) There are usually two or three <u>buttons</u>. When the pointer is over an icon, menu item, or the edge of a picture, the mouse buttons can be <u>clicked</u> or <u>double-clicked</u> to give the computer a <u>command</u>. A button can also be <u>held down</u> to <u>drag</u> something across the screen.

2) Mice tell the computer the <u>direction and speed</u> they are pushed. This is used to move the <u>pointer</u> on the <u>screen</u>. Optical mice have an optical sensor underneath and work out their movement by <u>watching</u> how the surface below them moves. Older mice use a <u>ball</u>. The ball <u>rotates</u> when the mouse is moved and <u>sensors</u> measure the movement of the ball in two directions.

Laptops usually have touch pads or trackerballs

1) <u>Touch-sensitive pads</u> look like <u>small screens</u>. You move your <u>finger</u> across the pad to move the <u>pointer</u>. They use <u>less space</u> than a mouse but usually don't work if you wear <u>gloves</u>, making them unsuitable for many scientific environments.

2) A <u>trackerball</u> works in the same way as a ball mouse, but the ball's moved <u>by hand</u>, so it takes up less space. Most people find using them a bit <u>fiddly</u>, and not that accurate or quick.

3) <u>Pointing sticks</u> are worked by putting a finger on them and pushing in some direction, which moves the pointer. They're really really small, not very accurate, and a bit weird.

Graphics Tablets make Drawing Easier and More Accurate

1) <u>Graphics tablets</u> (sometimes called <u>digitisers</u>) are like a pen and paper. They're made of a <u>touch-sensitive</u> surface (like the piece of paper) and a rigid <u>stylus</u> (like the pen).

2) The user presses on the surface with the stylus, and the touch-sensitive pad registers its <u>position</u>, and displays it on the <u>screen</u>.

touch-sensitive surface

rigid stylus

Learn loads of facts about the mouse? — what a drag...

Nothing too tricky here. But make sure you know the <u>difference</u> between both types of keyboard and all of the types of mouse. <u>And</u> you've got to know their <u>benefits and problems</u>.

Input Devices

Four more input devices for you to get excited about. Make <u>sure</u> you know how they work.

A Joystick can Input Movement

1) These are mainly used to play <u>computer games</u> — but they can also be used to move a computer-controlled device such as a <u>robot</u> or a <u>hospital body scanner</u>.

2) The joystick is fixed to a base but can be moved in <u>any</u> direction. The computer gets information from <u>sensors</u> on the joystick, which tells the computer how to update the <u>screen display</u> or move a <u>robot device</u>.

Use the smart bomb.
Use the smart bomb.

Scanners Convert Images into Digital Data

1) A scanner <u>converts</u> pictures into digital data — different parts of the picture are given different codes depending on their <u>colour</u> and <u>brightness</u>. The computer then builds up a '<u>map</u>' of the information based on these individual '<u>bits</u>' of data.

2) A problem is that these <u>bitmap files</u> can be very large and so take up a lot of <u>memory</u>. A benefit is that the scanned image can be <u>manipulated</u> and <u>edited</u> easily and quickly.

3) Most scanners are <u>flat-bed</u> devices, which are usually a few centimetres tall and slightly larger than an <u>A4</u> piece of paper.

OCR Software can Read Text

1) OCR stands for <u>Optical Character Recognition</u>. OCR software takes scanned digital information and looks for familiar <u>patterns</u> that might make up <u>letters or numbers</u>.

2) The software then creates a text file that can be <u>edited</u> using word-processing software.

3) This makes it quick and easy to enter <u>large blocks of text</u>. But the software is not <u>perfect</u>, so the result needs to be <u>proof-read</u>.

Don't forget OMR for Registers

1) OMR (<u>Optical Mark Recognition</u>) is used in some schools to take the class <u>register</u>.

2) The teacher fills in different boxes with a pencil if a pupil is present or absent. A <u>scanner</u> then reads the carbon in the boxes.

3) The system is <u>quick</u> and <u>accurate</u> — but only if the OMR sheet is filled in properly.

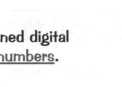

y Darbishire
ash
Park
Little
Rogers
Thompson

Cards use a Chip or a Magnetic Stripe on the Back

1) Chip and PIN cards have a computer <u>chip</u> which stores account information and the card's PIN number (in encrypted form). To use the card, the customer has to enter their PIN, which is checked against the PIN stored on the chip.

2) Before chips, account information was stored in a short length of <u>magnetic tape</u> sealed onto the back of the card.

3) All new cards have chips, and many also have a <u>magnetic stripe</u> for use with older tills.

interface to chip

magnetic stripe

8142 0000 6519 0000
MS C THOMPSON
18-23-05   08/07 08/10

Don't scan this page — read it slowly...

The danger with some of these pages is that you're going to think "Yeah, I know that," and not read it all carefully. But <u>don't</u> get <u>complacent</u> — make sure you know it all <u>properly</u>.

Input Devices

The last page of input devices. Look — it's the only rainbow page in the book. You've got to read it.

There are (Only) Nine More Input Devices

1 **DIGITAL CAMERAS** are a bit like scanners. They save an image as a series of dots called pixels. The image can then be uploaded to a computer and edited using photo-editing software. Most digital cameras can also record video clips, but dedicated video cameras are a better bet if you're going to be recording a lot of video footage.
Benefits — photographic film is not needed and the image is available for immediate use.
It can also be sent via an e-mail attachment to anywhere in the world.
Problem — high-resolution images use lots of memory.

2 **WEB CAMS** are basically digital cameras, but are usually used to take pictures and video footage that's going to be sent via the Internet.

3 **BAR-CODE READERS** are used in supermarkets and libraries.
They are used to read a bar code which contains data about the product being scanned.
Benefits — it makes buying goods faster and reduces the chance of human error.
Problems — the system is expensive and depends on the data in the bar code and the computer system being accurate.

4 **TOUCH SCREENS** are a bit like concept keyboards — but instead of pressing a key, you touch the picture or word on the screen. They're used a lot in information centres and quiz machines in pubs.
Benefits — easy to use and you can have different options each time the screen display changes.
Problems — more expensive than a keyboard, and they get dirty and sticky from being touched.

5 **MICROPHONES** are becoming increasingly used as an input device.
They are used to input data into voice-recognition systems, which convert sound into text or commands for the computer. They are also used to record sound so it can be stored digitally and sent over the Internet.
Benefit — you can use dictation instead of having to type.
Problem — sound data uses a lot of memory.

Yes, that's a microphone.

6 **SENSORS** are hardware that record environmental information and convert it to computer data.
Examples include temperature sensors, light sensors and infrared sensors used in burglar alarm systems. Sensors will be covered in the section on data logging.

7 **MIDI INSTRUMENTS** These instruments can be used to enter music into a computer package, e.g. a keyboard can be played and the notes recorded on the computer, where they can be edited.
Benefit — the sound of the notes can be changed easily, e.g. from a piano sound to a saxophone sound.
Problem — the computer software can be expensive.

8 **REMOTE CONTROLS** allow you to control devices like TVs, DVD and music players, and video games from a short distance away. They usually work using infrared radiation.

9 **INTERACTIVE WHITEBOARDS** look (at first) like normal, low-tech whiteboards that you can only write on with a pen. But in reality, they're fancy hi-tech things that are attached to a computer. The output from a computer (that would normally be shown on a monitor) can be projected onto the whiteboard. And the whiteboard also works like a touchscreen, allowing you to use your finger or a pen like a mouse pointer.

Image-Grabbing — don't do it in your local art gallery...

Phew, that's a load of input devices to remember. And you've got to know all their details.
Make a table with headings for device, how it works, benefits and problems. Then fill it in, as best you can. Keep trying until you get it absolutely perfect, or get so fed up that you pass out.

Output Devices — Printers

An <u>output device</u> is any hardware used to <u>communicate the result</u> of data processing.
<u>Printers</u> are used to produce a <u>permanent hard copy</u> of the information on paper.

Laser Printers are Ace but Expensive

Laser printers work in a very similar way to <u>photocopiers</u>. They have <u>four main parts</u>:

1) <u>Electrostatic rotating drum</u> — has an <u>electrical charge</u>.
2) <u>Laser</u> — 'etches' onto the drum a <u>negative image</u> of a page by <u>removing</u> electrical charge.
3) <u>Toner cartridge</u> — contains <u>ink</u>. As the drum passes over the toner cartridge, ink is <u>attracted</u> to charged areas of the drum, and then <u>transferred</u> onto the paper.
4) <u>Fuser unit</u> — <u>heats the paper</u> to <u>fuse the ink</u> onto it.

ADVANTAGES	DISADVANTAGES
<u>Very high resolution</u> — typically 600 dots per inch (dpi) or more, so they can print high-quality documents. <u>Very fast</u> — over 10 pages per minute (ppm). Laser printers are <u>very quiet</u>.	<u>Expensive</u> — though they're getting cheaper. Lots of <u>complex equipment</u> inside — so <u>expensive to repair</u>.

Inkjet Printers are a Popular Choice

1) These are the <u>cheapest</u> kind of printer, but they can produce good quality output.
   2) The main component is the <u>printhead</u>. This has lots of tiny <u>nozzles</u> or <u>spouts</u> through which small <u>jets</u> of ink are <u>sprayed</u> onto the paper.
   3) There are three different ways of controlling the flow of ink.
      i) The nozzles can be controlled by <u>crystals</u> inside the printhead, which <u>change shape</u> when an electrical current is passed through them.
      ii) The <u>ink can be heated</u> so that it <u>expands</u> and <u>pushes through</u> the nozzles.
      iii) <u>Continuous flow</u> printers <u>squirt ink continuously</u> from the nozzles, then <u>unused ink</u> is <u>electrically charged</u> and diverted back by charged plates.

ADVANTAGES	DISADVANTAGES
<u>Good resolution</u> — usually 300 to 600 dots per inch (dpi), so can print good quality documents. <u>Cheap to buy</u> — the cheapest are under £30. <u>Small</u> — so ideal for home desk use.	<u>Slow(ish)</u> — colour printing often less than <u>4 ppm</u>. <u>Expensive to run</u> — the <u>cartridges cost more</u> (per page) than laser printer cartridges.

Buffering and Spooling Help make Printing Easier

Computers process data <u>faster</u> than printers can print it. There are <u>two ways</u> to prevent <u>hold-ups</u>:

1) A <u>printer buffer</u> is <u>memory</u> that stores the pages that have not yet been printed. It is found inside the printer. This means the user can do other things while waiting for the printed document.

2) <u>Spooling</u> is when the document to be printed is <u>saved</u> onto the <u>hard disk</u> before being held in a <u>print queue</u>. This <u>frees up the CPU</u> to continue processing data. Again, this means the user can get on with <u>other tasks</u> without waiting for the printer.

Buy our printers — they're ace, but they cost a fortune...

Because of the differences between the printers, they're all suited to <u>different situations</u>.
Choose an <u>inkjet</u> if you want good quality, affordable printing — but not a lot of it.
Choose a <u>laser</u> if you want to print loads of pages of professional quality documents quickly.

Other Kinds of Output Device

Here are the rest of the main output devices. You need to know <u>how</u> each one works and <u>when</u> it should be used. Got that... good... off you go then.

Monitors give a Visual Display

<u>Monitors</u> are the most commonly used output device.

1) They're used when visual information is needed but a permanent record isn't.

2) Most monitors these days are flat-screen <u>LCD</u> models, but older computers used heavy, bulky cathode-ray tube (CRT) ones.

3) There are two important ways that monitors <u>differ</u> from each other — <u>size</u> and <u>resolution</u>.

\\\\ |||||||||||| | ||| //
Graphics designers and desktop
publishers who want to see a whole
design or page in great <u>detail</u> should
use a <u>large, high-resolution monitor</u>.
///| ||| ||||||||||| | |||

  i) <u>Size</u> — measured in inches across the <u>diagonal</u>. A typical general PC monitor has a size of at least <u>19 inches</u>. Most laptops have a screen about 15 inches across.

  ii) <u>Resolution</u> — measured by the number of <u>pixels</u> or <u>dots</u> that make up the image viewed on the screen. Most new monitors can show at least 1280×1024 pixels.

Graph Plotters are Specialised Printers

1) <u>Page (laser) printers</u> are good for most things but they're often <u>not accurate enough</u> for <u>precision drawings</u> such as architects' plans — and they can't print on big enough bits of paper.

2) The <u>most common</u> type of graph plotter is a <u>flatbed plotter</u>. The <u>paper</u> lies on a <u>flat surface</u> and a <u>plotter arm</u> moves over it from <u>left to right</u>. On the plotter arm is a <u>pen holder</u> which moves up and down the piece of paper. In this way the pen can draw <u>accurate lines</u> in any direction.

3) As colour page (laser) printers get <u>cheaper</u> and <u>better</u> there will be <u>less demand</u> for <u>small graph plotters</u>.

Speakers Output Sound

1) Computer speakers (especially the ones built into <u>laptops</u>) may not be the best quality possible.

2) New speakers can easily be attached to improve sound <u>quality</u> or <u>volume</u>.

Digital Projectors Show Output on a Big Screen

1) <u>Digital projectors</u> are used to project output that would normally appear on a monitor onto a big <u>cinema-style screen</u> (or a <u>wall</u>) instead.

2) They're useful if you have to present information to <u>large numbers</u> of people.

3) They're fairly <u>light</u> and <u>portable</u>, but can be quite <u>delicate</u> and easy to break.

1. Learn this stuff.
2. Fill your brain.

Output devices have come a long way since the cat flap...

Without some way to display their output to a user, computers aren't much more than <u>doorstops</u>. But still... doorstops with a 250 GB hard drive and a dual core processor... awesome.

Other Kinds of Output Device

As promised — the <u>final</u> page of output devices. But not boring, run-of-the-mill output devices like printers and monitors. No, this page is about robots and stuff. Well sort of, anyway.

Computers can Control External Devices

1) All output devices are activated by <u>signals</u> which come originally from the CPU. These signals can be used to control devices outside the computer.

2) For example, computer signals can switch things like <u>lights</u> and <u>buzzers</u> on and off. You just need a <u>control interface</u> to connect these output devices to the computer.

3) On their own, lights and buzzers aren't massively exciting. But if you string a few of them together and add an appropriate input device (e.g. a motion sensor), you can end up with a <u>burglar alarm system</u>, for example.

If only I'd paid some attention to lessons on output devices at school.

Actuators Can be Made to Move

A <u>control interface</u> can also be used to operate <u>actuators</u> — output devices that are able to move and perform simple mechanical tasks. There are <u>three main types of actuator</u>.

1) **MOTORS** are powered by an electricity supply.

   a) <u>STEPPER-MOTORS</u> are ones where the motor moves in a series of tiny but accurate steps. Flat-bed scanners are usually powered by stepper-motors.

   b) <u>SERVO-MOTORS</u> are ones where the motor moves continuously at high speed. These are used in computer-operated drills, for example.

When are they going to invent a stepper motor?

2) **HYDRAULIC ACTUATORS** are powered by <u>liquid pressure</u> controlled by the computer. This makes them <u>slow</u> but very <u>powerful</u>, so they're useful for heavy lifting equipment.

3) **PNEUMATIC ACTUATORS** are like hydraulic ones but are powered by <u>air pressure</u> instead. They're <u>less powerful</u> than hydraulic systems but <u>more responsive</u>, and are often used to power robots on fast-moving automated production lines.

Robotic Arms are a Type of Output Device

1) Once you can use a computer to control <u>physical movement</u>, the world is your oyster. This is because it's only a small step from that to things like <u>robotic arms</u>, and more...

2) Take a <u>computer</u>, some <u>actuators</u>, and connect them up using a few gears, levers and the like, and you have a device that can <u>grip</u> an object. Or, if your engineering skills are more advanced, you can build a device that can build a <u>car</u> — the principle is essentially the same.

Pneumatic actuators are like politicians — full of hot air...

Output devices are pretty important, otherwise you'd never know what your computer's thinking. You can pretty well <u>guarantee</u> you're going to be asked about them somewhere in the exam. If I were in your shoes, I reckon I'd be cramming this stuff into my brain for all I was worth.

Storage Devices — ROM and RAM

ROM and RAM are two types of computer <u>memory</u>. They're similar but different.

RAM is Temporary Memory

1) RAM is short for <u>Random-Access Memory</u>.
It's memory that can be read from or written to.

2) There are two types of RAM — <u>volatile</u> and <u>non-volatile</u>.

3) Volatile RAM keeps its contents only while <u>power</u> is supplied to it.
If you cut off the power then anything that's stored in it is <u>lost</u>.

4) Non-volatile RAM needs power to <u>change</u> its contents, but things
that are stored in it stay there even if the power is <u>switched off</u>.

It's the shepherd's next move.
Fear is in his heart.
He knows that ram's volatile.

5) Lots of people confuse <u>RAM</u> and the <u>hard drive</u>, but they're different. Hard drives are a <u>permanent</u>
data store, while RAM is a <u>temporary</u> store of data that the computer can access <u>more quickly</u>.

But if a computer doesn't have as much RAM as the computer would like to use (e.g. while
running lots of programs) then it'll use the hard drive as a kind of '<u>overflow</u>' memory — but data
stored there will be <u>much slower to access</u>. That's why adding more RAM to a computer can
influence its <u>processing power</u>, <u>speed</u>, and <u>how many</u> programs it can run at the same time.

ROM is Permanent Memory

1) ROM is short for <u>Read-Only Memory</u> — it's <u>permanent memory</u> and won't be lost
in a power cut, so it's a type of <u>non-volatile memory</u>. The amount of ROM in most
computers is <u>small</u> compared with the amount of RAM.

2) ROM contains the instructions that enable the <u>operating system</u> to be loaded into
RAM from the <u>backing store</u> (i.e. hard drives etc.) when the computer is switched on.

3) However, sometimes the computer <u>operating system</u> is stored on ROM.
This is especially true for mobile devices, like phones and PDAs (see page 2).

Data is stored in Bytes

1) Computers consist of a number of electric <u>circuits</u>, and each circuit must either be <u>on</u> or <u>off</u>.

2) This is why computers use a <u>binary code</u> (i.e. they use only 2 digits) to represent data.
Usually, a circuit that's switched <u>on</u> represents <u>1</u>, and a circuit that's switched <u>off</u> represents <u>0</u>.

Bit	Each individual 1 or 0 is called a <u>bit</u> — short for <u>binary digit</u>.
Byte	<u>8 bits</u> is called a <u>byte</u>.
Kilobyte	<u>1 kilobyte</u> (1 KB, or simply 1 K) is about a <u>thousand</u> bytes. To be exact, 1 KB = 2^{10} = 1024 bytes.
Megabyte	<u>1 megabyte</u> (1 MB) is about a <u>million</u> bytes (it's actually 2^{20} = 1048576 bytes).
Gigabyte	<u>1 gigabyte</u> (1 GB) is about a <u>thousand million</u> bytes (it's actually 2^{30} bytes).
Terabyte	<u>1 terabyte</u> (1 TB) is about a <u>million million</u> bytes (it's actually 2^{40} bytes).

Morse code works in
a similar way — it's
either a dot or a dash.

This is all just data-day stuff...

Well there you are. Make sure you learn the difference between **ROM** and **RAM**. And that there
are eight bits in every byte. Remember the way to learn — <u>study</u> the page, <u>understand</u> it — then
<u>memorise</u> it and <u>write the key points</u> down. And if you get any bits wrong, do it all again. Easy.

Data Storage — Backing Storage

A backing store (also known as a secondary store) is any data-storage area that the CPU uses outside of its ROM and RAM. And the good news is, there are lots and lots of types to learn.

Hard Disks are the Main Data Store

1) Hard disks are usually found inside computers. They're stacks of magnetised circular metal plates. Each plate is divided into concentric tracks and sectors — and data is stored in the sectors (usually on both sides of the individual plates).

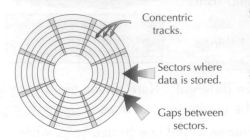

Concentric tracks.

Sectors where data is stored.

Gaps between sectors.

2) Read/write heads float just above the surface of the disk. They're so close that a speck of dust would ruin the hard drive — so the disk drive is kept in a sealed unit.

3) Hard drives are usually housed inside a computer. However, you can also get external hard drives for additional storage — these are also useful if a hard drive needs to be swapped between different computers.

4) The main benefit of hard drives is that they have a large capacity — hundreds or thousands of gigabytes (1 gigabyte = 1024 megabytes) are now common. But if there's a problem with the hard drive, all of the data stored on it may be lost.

Solid-State Drives are a More Robust Alternative

1) Solid-state drives perform the same function as a hard drive, but they have no moving parts, so they're not affected by movement or shocks. This makes them ideal for use in mobile devices.

2) They also have quick access times (i.e. they can read data very quickly).

3) However, they're more expensive (per unit of storage) than a hard drive.

Optical Discs are the Main External Backing Store

Optical discs include Compact Discs (CDs) and Digital Versatile Discs (DVDs). They store digital data as pits (i.e. little indentations) on the surface of a reflective disc. The data is read by moving a laser beam across the surface of the disc and reading the change in position of the reflected beam.

There are three different types of CD:

1) CD-ROMs hold around 650 megabytes, but you can't write to them (see p9 for more on ROM).

2) CD-Rs (the R stands for 'recordable') are sold as blank CDs, and can have data written onto them... but only once. After that they work in the same way as CD-ROMs. Both CD-ROMs and CD-Rs are known as WORM discs — "Write Once and Read Many times".

3) CD-RWs are also available. RW stands for Re-Writable. They're like a CD-R but can have old data deleted and new data written onto the disc.

DVDs are like CDs but hold much more data — up to 8.54 gigabytes a side. As a result they can store whole films digitally. You can get DVD-ROMs, DVD±Rs and DVD±RWs. These work in the same way as CD-ROMs, CD-Rs and CD-RWs. DVD-RAMs are like DVD±RWs but are made to be more suitable for frequent updating and changing of data than either DVD±RWs or CD-RWs.

Blu-Ray™ discs are like DVDs but again hold much more data — nearly 6 times as much as a standard DVD. They're used for storing films in high definition.

Optical discs — that's what I call the lenses in my specs...

The above are types of "backing storage". Don't get this confused with "backing up", which means making a copy of data in case the original gets lost or destroyed. See the next page for more info.

Data Storage — Backing Storage

Wonderful news — there are three more types of backing storage for you to enjoy.
Once again, make sure you know <u>how</u> each one works and <u>what</u> its uses are.

Flash Memory is a Type of Solid-State Drive...

1) Flash memory is a type of <u>non-volatile</u> memory which can be used to store <u>gigabytes</u> of data.

2) Flash memory is a lot <u>slower</u> than the computer's main RAM, but is often <u>faster</u> than a hard disk.

3) It's very stable and doesn't break easily. It does 'wear out' eventually, though.

...and is used in Memory Sticks and Memory Cards

1) Flash memory's often sold in <u>pen-sized devices</u> that you can easily connect to your computer using a <u>USB</u> socket (so they're often referred to as pen drives, memory sticks or USB drives).

USB stands for Universal Serial Bus — it's a standard connection that most computers support.

2) They allow you to easily <u>transfer</u> data between computers.

3) Some operating systems, such as Windows® 7, even let you use memory sticks as a <u>temporary storage area</u> between RAM and the hard disk. That can lead to a faster computer.

4) The main disadvantages are that they are <u>easily lost</u> or stolen.

5) Flash memory is also used to make small <u>memory cards</u>. They come in lots of different shapes and sizes, but most are close to rectangular and about the size of a <u>coin</u>.

6) Memory cards are used by <u>digital cameras</u> and some <u>mobile phones</u> and <u>MP3 players</u>. Many computers come with slots for memory cards, which means that you can use them for reading and writing files just like a <u>memory stick</u>.

Magnetic Tape can Back Up Large Amounts of Data

1) <u>Magnetic tape</u> is often used when large amounts of data need to be backed up.

> <u>Backing up</u> means making <u>copies</u> of files that can be stored somewhere <u>safe</u>.
> The idea is that they can be used if the <u>original</u> gets <u>lost</u> or <u>damaged</u> for some reason.
> Back-ups need to be kept <u>secure</u> — ideally in <u>locked fireproof rooms</u> in a <u>different location</u>.

2) With magnetic tape, data is written to and read from tape in the same way as in a <u>video recorder</u>.

3) Very large amounts of data can be stored relatively <u>cheaply</u>.

4) However, <u>access time</u> is <u>slow</u>, because the <u>read/write head</u> can't go directly to a particular piece of data — you have to wind through the whole tape. This is called <u>serial</u> or <u>sequential access</u>. In contrast, disk drives and flash memory give <u>direct access</u> to data — much handier.

On-line Storage is Good For Backing Up and Easy Access

1) <u>On-line storage</u> means storing data on the file servers of an ISP, an Internet Service Provider (see p53 for more info), instead of on your own computer's hard disk.

2) You can use on-line storage to: <u>back up</u> your files
   <u>share</u> your files with other people (e.g. holiday photos)
   <u>access</u> your files from <u>any</u> computer with Internet access

Back up — the type of putting you apply to fallen things...

All good things must come to an end — including two pages of backing storage devices.
Study the two pages carefully, then list <u>how they work</u>, and the <u>advantages and disadvantages</u>.

Revision Summary for Section One

Section One is pretty important, I reckon. It gives you all the information you need on the bits and bobs that make up a computer system. And now you've learnt all the stuff, it's time to test yourself with some fiendishly tricky questions — so you can see how much of this stuff you've really understood. This might all sound a bit scary, but then again, it's better to find out what you don't know now, rather than in the middle of your GCSE exam. That way you can do something about it. So your basic aim is to get every question right — even if it takes you a couple of attempts.

1) What's a CPU? Where would you find one inside a computer?

2) What is a mainframe? What's an embedded computer? What about a supercomputer?

3) What's the difference between hardware and software?

4) Describe: a) a laptop, b) a netbook, c) a PDA

5) Explain the difference between a smartphone and a "normal" mobile phone.

6) What are the first six letters on a normal keyboard?

7) How are concept keyboards different?

8) Describe how a mouse works.

9) Explain one difference between a touch-sensitive pad and a mouse.

10) What type of file is created when an image is put through a scanner?

11) What do the letters OCR and OMR stand for? What do they mean?

12) List five other input devices — and explain how they work.

13) Dozy Doris has been asked to perform the following tasks. For each one list the input device that she should use:
    a) type text to create a letter,
    b) record a sound message to appear on a website,
    c) take a photo of herself and e-mail it to a friend.

14) How does a laser printer work? Give two advantages and one disadvantage of laser printers compared to inkjet printers.

15) Why are inkjets the most popular printers for home use?

16) What is the difference between buffering and spooling? Why is each one useful?

17) What are two main ways that monitors differ from each other?

18) Explain what a digital projector does.

19) What are the three main types of actuator called? How do they differ from each other?

20) What is the difference between ROM and RAM?

21) Explain the terms: a) bit, b) byte, c) megabyte, d) terabyte

22) What is a hard disk? How do they work?

23) What does WORM mean? Give the name of two types of WORM discs.

24) What's so flash about flash memory? And what is flash memory used for?

25) Which method is quicker when accessing data — serial or direct access? Why?

26) Give three uses for on-line data storage.

Operating Systems

The <u>Operating System</u> (<u>OS</u>) is the <u>software</u> that enables <u>applications</u> and the rest of the computer system to work. The most popular types of OS are <u>Windows</u>®; <u>Mac OS</u>®; and <u>Linux</u>.

There are Different Types of Operating System

All OSs have the <u>same function</u> — they <u>talk</u> to the various bits of a computer (see page 1) so applications and hardware can run properly. But there are <u>different ways</u> that an OS can work:

<u>Interactive</u> OSs, as the name suggests, allow users to <u>interact with</u> <u>programs</u> — they can <u>alter the result</u> of the program while it's running. This is different to some <u>older</u> and <u>specialised OSs</u>, where programs run <u>without</u> allowing the user to affect the final outcome.

The Windows® OS is interactive and multi-tasking.

<u>Multi-tasking</u> OSs can run many programs at the <u>same time</u>. That means that they have to <u>share out resources</u> such as the available memory and CPU time. If more than one program wants to communicate with a <u>peripheral</u> (e.g. if two programs want to access the Internet at once), then the OS has to make sure that's <u>shared too</u>.

<u>Multi-user</u> OSs allow <u>many people</u> to log into a computer and use it at the <u>same time</u>. A multi-user OS has to do similar <u>sharing of resources</u> to a multi-tasking OS. It also has to keep track of <u>multiple workspaces</u>, so that each user has the <u>same experience</u> as they would using an individual computer.

<u>Real time</u> OSs run programs that need to <u>react</u> in a specific amount of time to events occurring in the <u>outside world</u>, e.g. the stock markets or the weather. The OS manages the computer's resources so that programs <u>aren't interrupted</u>, allowing them to meet the <u>deadline</u> for their responses.

You might have heard about 'cloud computing' — online OSs are part of this.

<u>Online</u> OSs are stored on a <u>computer server</u> (see page 1) that doesn't belong to the user. Users' <u>files</u>, e.g. documents, pictures, and music, are <u>also stored</u> on the server. Users <u>log in</u> to the OS from any <u>Internet-enabled</u> computer — they can then use the OS as if it was on their own computer.

Drivers let Operating Systems Talk to Hardware

1) Drivers are <u>files</u> that tell OSs how to communicate with computer <u>hardware</u>.

2) Most <u>devices</u>, e.g. printers, come with a <u>disc</u> with suitable drivers on it (or some instructions giving you details of a webpage where you can <u>download</u> the drivers).

3) You need to <u>install</u> the driver on the computer that the device is hooked up to, so the OS knows <u>how</u> to speak to the new device and <u>make it work</u>.

We're off to see the wizard, the wonderful wizard of OS...

Dorothy: "I had a wonderful dream — and you were there, and you, and you. But there were a whole bunch of other people who wanted to use you, and I had to <u>share you out</u> fairly."

Operating Systems — Organisation of Data

I'm sure you've wondered how a system stores information, and how it keeps track of where it all is...

Data is Stored in Files and Directories

1) A file is a block of data that's stored under one name, called its filename
— e.g. a picture file, or a letter written on a word processor.

2) Some OSs store extra information with the file to identify its type and which program should be used to open it. In Windows®, this information is usually just an extension (an extra bit at the end of a filename). E.g. Microsoft® Word documents have the extension .doc or .docx.

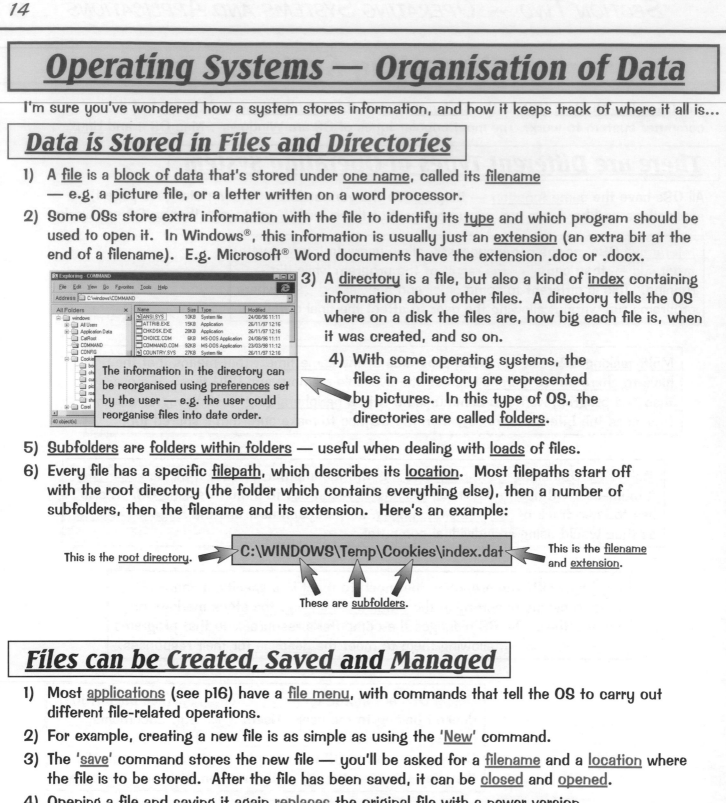

3) A directory is a file, but also a kind of index containing information about other files. A directory tells the OS where on a disk the files are, how big each file is, when it was created, and so on.

The information in the directory can be reorganised using preferences set by the user — e.g. the user could reorganise files into date order.

4) With some operating systems, the files in a directory are represented by pictures. In this type of OS, the directories are called folders.

5) Subfolders are folders within folders — useful when dealing with loads of files.

6) Every file has a specific filepath, which describes its location. Most filepaths start off with the root directory (the folder which contains everything else), then a number of subfolders, then the filename and its extension. Here's an example:

This is the root directory. → `C:\WINDOWS\Temp\Cookies\index.dat` ← This is the filename and extension.

These are subfolders.

Files can be Created, Saved and Managed

1) Most applications (see p16) have a file menu, with commands that tell the OS to carry out different file-related operations.

2) For example, creating a new file is as simple as using the 'New' command.

3) The 'save' command stores the new file — you'll be asked for a filename and a location where the file is to be stored. After the file has been saved, it can be closed and opened.

4) Opening a file and saving it again replaces the original file with a newer version. The 'save as' command lets you save a copy of the file, while keeping the original.

File management operations controlled by the OS include:

- Renaming — changing the filename of a file.
- Deleting — removing a stored file.
- Moving — transferring the file to a new location (so it has a new filepath).
- Copying — making a duplicate of the file.

File › New Joke...

You're probably used to navigating around folders and files on a computer — this is just some of the theory behind it. It's not really complicated, but make sure you know this page inside out.

Operating Systems — User Interfaces

A <u>user interface</u> is the posh term for the way the user communicates with the OS, or other software.

Some User Interfaces use Command-Lines...

1) A <u>command-line interface</u> presents the user with a blank screen. The user types in <u>commands</u> which the OS then carries out.

2) It can take a <u>long time</u> to learn all the commands you're likely to need, but the systems can be very <u>powerful</u>.

...but Most use a Graphical User Interface (or GUI)

1) These are the most popular types of user interface — all major modern operating systems use them. A GUI combines a <u>menu-driven</u> interface with <u>icons</u> to represent the main commands.

2) GUIs are <u>more intuitive</u> and <u>accessible</u> than command-line interfaces. For example, <u>menus</u> display lists of commands or options that are selected by clicking them with a mouse, and moving a file is as easy as <u>dragging and dropping</u> it in its new location.

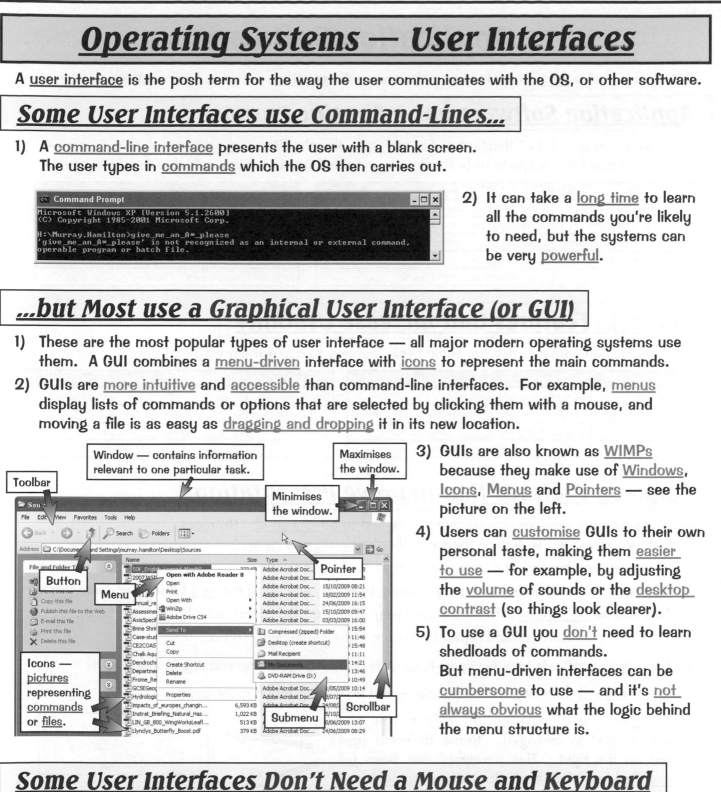

3) GUIs are also known as <u>WIMPs</u> because they make use of <u>Windows</u>, <u>Icons</u>, <u>Menus</u> and <u>Pointers</u> — see the picture on the left.

4) Users can <u>customise</u> GUIs to their own personal taste, making them <u>easier to use</u> — for example, by adjusting the <u>volume</u> of sounds or the <u>desktop contrast</u> (so things look clearer).

5) To use a GUI you <u>don't</u> need to learn shedloads of commands. But menu-driven interfaces can be <u>cumbersome</u> to use — and it's <u>not always obvious</u> what the logic behind the menu structure is.

Some User Interfaces Don't Need a Mouse and Keyboard

1) Many user interfaces are controlled using input devices like mice and keyboards, but <u>modern technology</u> has started to move away from them.

2) <u>Touch-screens</u>, e.g. in some mobile phones and tablet PCs, allow users to <u>press</u> the device's screen to select options or drag items around.

3) A person's <u>voice</u> can also control software — many mobile phones have <u>voice-activated dialling</u>.

4) <u>Direct neural interfacing</u> is all about controlling a computer with your <u>brain</u>. Very futuristic.

A GUI touch-screen would make your fingers all sticky...

Please stop laughing at my excellent jokes, there's <u>revision</u> to be done. GUIs are <u>all over the place</u> in modern-day computing, but don't forget about the humble <u>command-line interface</u> when revising.

Application Software

This stuff is just a <u>intro</u> to application software — the <u>specifics</u> are all in later sections.

Application Software has a Specific Purpose

Computers can do a lot of things, but for <u>each task</u> there's often a <u>specific piece of software</u> — just as you don't use a spade to butter toast, you don't use database software to edit images:

Application software	Used for...
Spreadsheet software	Calculating and analysing <u>data</u>.
Database software	Storing large amounts of <u>data</u>.
Word processing software	<u>Documents</u>, e.g. letters.
Desktop publishing software	Documents with a <u>flexible layout</u>, e.g. magazines.
Presentation software	<u>Slides</u> of information to show to people.

Application software	Used for making...
Web design software	<u>Websites</u>
Audio & video software	<u>Music</u> and <u>videos</u>
Graphics software	<u>Images</u>
Animation software	<u>Moving images</u> (2D or 3D)
Programming software	Other <u>software</u>. Crazy.

Common Features that Increase Usability

Most application software has the same basic features to make them <u>easier to use</u>:

Feature	What it does
Undo/Redo	<u>Reverses</u> or <u>repeats</u> an action.
Cut, copy and paste	<u>Moves</u> things, e.g. text, from one place to another.
Wizards	<u>Walks the user through</u> a complicated action.
Help files	<u>Instructs</u> users on how to use the software.

Feature	What it does
Drag and drop	Makes <u>moving things</u> around dead easy.
Find and replace	<u>Searches</u> for specific things and <u>changes</u> them.
Zoom	<u>Enlarges</u> a <u>specific area</u> of a document.
Printing	Creates a <u>hard copy</u> of the data in a file.

Common Features that Improve Presentation

Most applications produce <u>output</u> that's designed to be <u>looked at</u>. So most applications allow you to <u>format</u> things so they're <u>pretty</u> and <u>clear</u>.

1) <u>Fonts</u> can be changed, e.g. from Arial to Times New Roman.

2) <u>Text size</u> can be changed, e.g. emphasising <u>headings</u> and <u>sub-headings</u> by making them <u>larger</u>

3) Text can be <u>highlighted</u>. There are four ways to make text stand out. Words can be in:

　　　(i) **bold type**,　(ii) *italics,*　(iii) <u>underlined,</u>　(iv) colour.

4) <u>Line spacing</u> adjusts how far apart lines of text are. Double-line spacing is much

　　<u>easier to read</u> than single-line spacing — but it uses up much <u>more paper</u>.

5) <u>Alignment</u> and <u>justification</u> affect how each line of text is arranged. Some different types are on the right. This paragraph has been <u>fully justified</u>, so that each line is the <u>same length</u>.

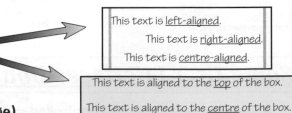

This text is <u>left-aligned</u>.
　　　This text is <u>right-aligned</u>.
This text is <u>centre-aligned</u>.

This text is aligned to the <u>top</u> of the box.

This text is aligned to the <u>centre</u> of the box.

This text is aligned to the <u>bottom</u> of the box.

6) <u>Headers</u> (top of a page) and <u>footers</u> (bottom of a page) show useful information, e.g. <u>titles</u>, <u>dates</u>, and <u>page numbers</u>.

7) A page's <u>orientation</u> can be either <u>portrait</u> (tall and narrow) or <u>landscape</u> (short and wide).

8) <u>Margins</u> are <u>blank</u> areas at the edges of pages — they can help 'frame' a page's contents.

9) <u>Inserting images</u> in a document can help make a page <u>more attractive</u> and <u>clearer</u>. Text can then be <u>wrapped</u> around an image (see p31).

Text justification — why use words...

Not many applications do more than one thing — they're usually very <u>specialised</u> bits of kit. But most of them share <u>common features</u>, to make your life (and revision) easier.

Everyday Tips and Problems

Try <u>not</u> to say 'yeah, yeah, whatever...' too much when reading this page
— it's quite <u>useful</u>, and it could well come up in your exam.

The Basics — Turning a Computer On and Off

1) When you <u>switch on</u> a computer it usually beeps and then <u>loads</u> the operating system — it'll stop loading if you need to <u>log on</u> to access your <u>account</u>.

2) <u>Logging on</u> to a computer requires a <u>user name</u> and <u>password</u>. It's important to <u>remember</u> these as you won't be able to use the computer if you can't log on.

If you can't remember your user name or password, speak to the person who looks after the computer accounts.

3) After you've <u>finished</u> using the computer you need to <u>shut it down</u>. <u>Don't</u> head straight for the socket and turn the power off — computers don't like this.

4) The best way to <u>shut down</u> a computer is by using a <u>menu</u>. Most operating systems give you a <u>few options</u> for this, such as...
   - <u>shut down</u> (turn the computer off),
   - <u>log off</u> (leave the computer on but let others log on),
   - <u>stand by</u> (the computer 'goes to sleep', reducing energy consumption).

Basic Hardware and Software Problems can be Solved

1) Computers sometimes <u>go wrong</u>. The problem could be serious, and an absolute nightmare to sort out. But very often, the problem can be made to go away quite simply.

2) For example, when <u>software freezes</u> (<u>stops responding</u> to a user's input), or a piece of <u>hardware</u> stops working, there are a few things you should try before you panic too much:

- <u>Restart your system</u> — this will sort a lot of problems out. If you can access the <u>shut down menu</u>, use it. Otherwise hold the computer's <u>power button</u> until it turns off.

- <u>Reinstall software</u> — if a program is <u>frequently not working</u>, you could try reinstalling it. A file might have been <u>corrupted</u>, so installing a <u>fresh version</u> may fix the problem.

- <u>Install patches</u> — if there's a problem with the <u>source code</u> (see page 42) of a program, a <u>programmer</u> might create a <u>patch</u> that fixes the problem. These are usually available from the manufacturer's website.

Have you tried restarting your computer...?

- <u>Check your hardware</u> — check that you've <u>connected</u> the hardware <u>correctly</u> and that it's <u>turned on</u>. Also make sure that you're not expecting your hardware to do the <u>impossible</u> — e.g. if you're writing data to a CD, make sure the CD has a big enough storage capacity.

- <u>Update drivers</u> — drivers let hardware <u>talk</u> to the operating system. Without the right drivers it might <u>seem</u> like your hardware is broken, <u>even if it's not</u>. Up-to-date drivers are usually available from the manufacturer's website.

3) A lot of other problems (e.g. paper jams in a printer) can be <u>solved easily</u> once you've read the <u>instructions</u> or have been <u>shown</u> what to do.

4) But if you <u>can't</u> sort a problem out on your own, you should always <u>get help</u> from a <u>trained person</u>, e.g. a teacher or ICT professional.

A critical error has occurred — re-read this page to continue...

OK, that seemed like I was stating the <u>obvious</u>, but there's every chance you'll get a question on this stuff — and you don't want to lose out on some marks because you <u>thought</u> you knew it all...

Revision Summary for Section Two

I know, you're upset that you've nearly finished another section and you're that little bit closer to finishing your revision. Don't worry though, I've got something that'll cheer you right up — a selection of questions to make sure you've understood everything on the last few pages. Hooray...

1) What is the main function of an operating system?

2) Describe the main feature of a multi-tasking operating system.

3) Describe the main feature of a multi-user operating system.

4) If a computer program has to run in fifteen seconds, no more and no less, what type of operating system should be used to run it?

5) What's so special about an online operating system?

6) Why do drivers have to be installed when you connect a new device to a computer?

7) What is a file?

8) On a PC using a Windows® operating system, where can you find out a file's type?

9) What is a subfolder?

10) What does a filepath describe?

11) Describe the difference between the 'save' command and the 'save as' command.

12) Describe three file operations that are carried out by an operating system.

13) How does a user control an operating system through a command-line interface?

14) Give one disadvantage of a command-line interface.

15) What does GUI stand for?

16) Describe two ways in which a GUI is more intuitive than a command-line interface.

17) Name four things that you would expect to see in a GUI.

18) Why do people customise their GUIs? Give one example of such a customisation.

19) Give one disadvantage of a GUI.

20) Describe two examples of how a user interface can be controlled without a mouse or keyboard.

21) What is desktop publishing software used to make?

22) What is programming software used to make?

23) Why are wizards helpful for users of applications software?

24) What feature allows users to view a specific area in an application?

25) Name three ways that text can be highlighted.

26) What's the difference between a header and a footer?

27) Explain the following terms: margins, justification, page orientation.

28) What's the correct way to turn off a computer?

29) Describe three fixes that you can try if you need to sort out a hardware or software problem.

Spreadsheets — The Basics

Most people find spreadsheets a bit scary — very few people really <u>understand</u> them. But they're basically pretty simple. Make sure you learn this page well before moving onto the trickier stuff.

Spreadsheets are Clever Calculators

1) A spreadsheet is simply a program that can <u>display</u> and <u>process</u> data in a <u>structured</u> way. Most people think spreadsheets can only process <u>numbers</u> — but they can handle <u>text</u> as well.

2) Spreadsheets can: a) <u>record</u> data,
                 b) <u>sort</u> data,
                 c) <u>search</u> for particular items of data,
                 d) <u>perform calculations</u> based on data,
                 e) produce <u>graphs</u> and <u>charts</u>.

> Data can be sorted in <u>ascending</u> (A to Z, 1 to 10) or <u>descending</u> (Z to A, 10 to 1) order. You can sort data by <u>column</u> and <u>row</u>.

3) <u>Examples</u> of uses include keeping records of patients in a doctor's surgery, calculating the exam results of a group of pupils, and producing graphs based on the results of a questionnaire.

Data is Entered into Cells

1) A spreadsheet is made up of tables. <u>Rows</u> and <u>columns</u> divide each table up into individual <u>cells</u>.

2) Each cell in a table can be identified using the column letter and row number as <u>coordinates</u>.

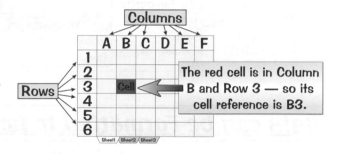

The red cell is in Column B and Row 3 — so its cell reference is B3.

Each Cell can Contain One of Three Things

Each cell can contain <u>one</u> (and only one) of three things...

NUMERICAL DATA	TEXT (or ALPHANUMERIC) DATA	FORMULAS
e.g. integers (whole numbers), fractions, numbers with decimal places, dates, times, money, percentages. Most spreadsheets recognise dates and money and convert them into a suitable number format, e.g. if you enter 23-6, it changes to 23 June.	e.g. people's names, titles of songs. 1) Column headings usually contain text. 2) One process that can be carried out on text is sorting it into alphabetical order. 3) The ICT term for a piece of text is a <u>text string</u>.	1) These allow results of calculations to be displayed inside a cell. 2) E.g. you could get the computer to add up all the numbers in a column and display the answer in a cell at the bottom of the column. 3) The great thing about spreadsheets is that if any numbers are changed, the results are automatically updated.

The <u>Golden Rule</u> is to put only one piece of data in a cell — this means that you shouldn't <u>mix</u> any of these types of data.

> Alphanumeric is just a fancy way of saying letters and numbers.

1) If you enter the weight of a kilo of fish as '1000g' then you have <u>numerical</u> data (1000) and <u>text</u> data (g).

2) Spreadsheets treat cells with <u>any text</u> in them as though they contain <u>only</u> text data.

3) This means the spreadsheet will read '1000g' as <u>text</u> — which means you <u>can't</u> do any calculations with it. Bummer.

The exceptions are things like currencies where the spreadsheet knows that £5 has a value of 5.

Take a recess — and learn about cells...

The best way to get to grips with spreadsheets (or any new kind of software) is to have a <u>play</u> with them. That goes for the rest of this section — try out the stuff you've learnt on a computer.

Spreadsheets — Entering Data

Now you know the basics, it's time for the <u>fun part</u> — putting the data in. No, really, it <u>is</u> fun...

Data can be Entered Directly or with Controls

Learn all this stuff about entering data and formatting a spreadsheet:

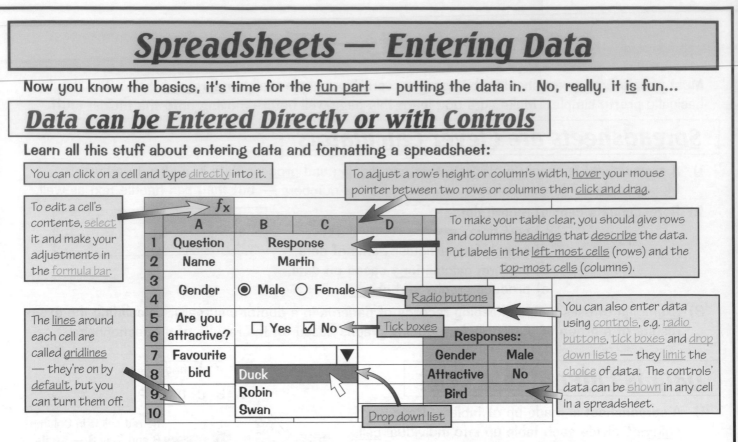

You can click on a cell and type <u>directly</u> into it.

To adjust a row's height or column's width, <u>hover</u> your mouse pointer between two rows or columns then <u>click and drag</u>.

To edit a cell's contents, <u>select</u> it and make your adjustments in the <u>formula bar</u>.

To make your table clear, you should give rows and columns <u>headings</u> that <u>describe</u> the data. Put labels in the <u>left-most cells</u> (rows) and the <u>top-most cells</u> (columns).

Radio buttons

Tick boxes

You can also enter data using <u>controls</u>, e.g. <u>radio buttons</u>, <u>tick boxes</u> and <u>drop down lists</u> — they <u>limit</u> the <u>choice</u> of data. The controls' data can be <u>shown</u> in any cell in a spreadsheet.

The <u>lines</u> around each cell are called <u>gridlines</u> — they're on by <u>default</u>, but you can turn them off.

Drop down list

Data can be Formatted to Improve its Appearance

1) Data in spreadsheets can be formatted in similar ways to a <u>word processor</u>. Use <u>italics</u>, <u>bold</u> type, different <u>fonts</u>, <u>colours</u>, <u>sizes</u> etc. to make data stand out.

2) The <u>alignment</u> of data can be changed — it's the usual suspects of left, right and centre aligned (<u>horizontal alignment</u>) and top, middle and bottom aligned (<u>vertical alignment</u>).

3) The <u>cells</u> containing the data can be <u>jazzed up</u> a little bit too. For example, different <u>fill colours</u> (or <u>shading</u>) can be applied to them, and <u>borders</u> of varying thicknesses can be drawn around them — these formatting options can help show data <u>more clearly</u>.

	A	B	C
1	ICT Club	membership fees owing	
2	First Name	Last Name	Amount owing
3	Teresa	Wood	£8.00
4	Tanya	Hide	£5.52
5	Arthur	Brain	£0.00
6	Willie	Winn	£0.00
7	Betty	Wont	£33.87

4) Some spreadsheets allow <u>conditional formatting</u>. The format of a cell is automatically changed if its contents meet certain <u>conditions</u>, like if a number's negative. Here, the cells turn red if the person owes money.

5) Cells can also be <u>merged</u> — <u>two or more cells</u> become <u>one cell</u>. It's useful for <u>labels</u> that apply to <u>more than one</u> row or column.

6) You might have noticed cells that store data in <u>one line</u> that goes on <u>forever</u> and ever and ever and...

To display data over <u>many lines</u>, you need to turn on the <u>text wrap</u> option — the data will fill up each line (as <u>wide as the cell</u>) and then start a new one. The cell will get <u>taller</u>, which means all other cells in that <u>row</u> also get taller. Which can be annoying...

7) If you're printing a spreadsheet, a useful feature to use is to print certain rows and columns on every page. This means you can show labels, making the print-out easier to read.

It takes me 15 minutes to format my face in the morning...

If you don't know this stuff already, get yourself on a computer, load up a spreadsheet and try doing all the things described on this page. It's all <u>good clean fun</u>.

Spreadsheets — Simple Formulas

Without formulas, spreadsheets are just fancy tables. Formulas put the <u>ace</u> into 'ace spreadsheet'.

A Formula is a Simple Computer Program

1) A <u>formula</u> is an instruction to the computer to <u>process</u> data held in specific cells.

STEP 1 — Click the cell where you want the <u>answer</u>.

STEP 2 — Type an <u>equals</u> sign (=). This tells the computer to expect a formula.

STEP 3 — Type in the <u>formula</u>.
Here, it would be <u>C3+D3+E3</u>.

	A	B	C	D	E	F
1	Exam Marks for 1st Year Mocks					
2	First Name	Last Name	Maths	ICT	English	Total
3	Teresa	Wood	63	45	89	=C3+D3+E3
4	Tanya	Hide	32	54	78	
5	Arthur	Brain	33	53	95	
6	Willie	Winn	24	54	75	
7	Betty	Wont	64	53	88	

2) Simple formulas contain normal maths symbols like +, –, * (for <u>multiply</u>) and / (for <u>divide</u>).

3) For more <u>complicated</u> calculations, spreadsheets usually have a range of built-in <u>functions</u> (e.g. AVERAGE and SINE). You can either type functions in, or choose them from a list.

4) Once you've entered a formula, you can <u>copy</u> it to other cells. So the formula in F3 could be copied to cells F4 to F7 — and the computer would automatically insert the correct formulas for the totals of these rows. This makes spreadsheets an easy way to do lots of <u>similar</u> calculations on a <u>large</u> set of data.

	C	D	E	F
1				
2	Maths	ICT	English	Total
3	63	45	89	=C3+D3+E3
4	32	54	78	=C4+D4+E4
5	33	53	95	=C5+D5+E5
6	24	54	75	=C6+D6+E6
7	64	53	88	=C7+D7+E7

5) Spreadsheets <u>recalculate formulas automatically</u> — e.g. if you change the data in a cell range used by a formula, the formula's result will be <u>updated</u> without you having to think about it.

Formulas can have Absolute or Relative Cell References

1) In the example above, the formula in F3 (=C3+D3+E3) tells the computer to add together the data in the three cells to the left. If you copy this formula to cell F4, it still adds together the contents of the three cells to the left, so F4 becomes '=C4+D4+E4'. That's why they're called <u>relative cell references</u> — the data used is in the same place <u>relative to the answer cell</u>.

2) Sometimes part of a formula always needs to refer to <u>one particular cell</u>. In this case, you need to use an <u>absolute cell reference</u> — one that won't be changed. The usual way to make a cell reference absolute is to put a <u>dollar sign</u> in front of each part of the cell's coordinates. So B12 is a relative cell reference — but B12 is an absolute cell reference.

Column C:
=B2 / 100 * C9
=B3 / 100 * C9
⋮

Column D:
=B2 – C2
=B3 – C3
⋮

3) The spreadsheet to the right uses an absolute cell reference (to represent the % commission a letting agency charges on its properties).

	A	B	C	D
1	Property	Monthly Rent	Letting Agent's comission	Amount to Landlord
2	Oak Vale	£450	£45	£405
3	The Old Post Office	£300	£30	£270
4	Ash House	£250	£25	£225
5	Lilac Cottage	£150	£15	£135
6	Low Wood	£500	£50	£450
7			£165	£1,485
8				
9	Letting Agent's Commission (%)		10	

Relative cell — we keep Granny in ours...

Make sure you understand <u>all</u> the formulas. You should be able to <u>write</u> them down as you'd <u>type</u> them. And you need to know the difference between <u>absolute</u> and <u>relative</u> cell references. Phew...

Spreadsheets — Functions

You'll need to know about the following functions that are found in most spreadsheet software.

Functions tell a Spreadsheet How to Process Data

Function	What it does...	Example	Result
SUM	Adds up numbers.	=SUM(C3:C7)	216
AVERAGE	Averages numbers — the mean average.	=AVERAGE(C3:C7)	43.2
ROUND	Rounds numbers to a specified number of decimal places.	=ROUND(43.2,0)	43
ROUNDUP	Same as ROUND, but only rounds up.	=ROUNDUP(43.2,0)	44
MAX	Finds the largest value in a cell range.	=MAX(C3:C7)	64
MIN	Finds the smallest value in a cell range.	=MIN(C3:C7)	24
RANK	Finds the position of a number in a range of numbers after it has been sorted in ascending (1) or descending order (0).	=RANK(C4,C3:C7,1)	2
		=RANK(C4,C3:C7,0)	4
COUNT	Counts the number of cells that contain only numbers (numerical data).	=COUNT(B2:C7)	5
IF	Checks if data matches a condition — result depends on the match being true or false.	=IF(C7>40,"Yes","No")	No

	A	B	C	D
1	Maths Exam Results			
2	First Name	Last Name	Mark	Pass?
3	Teresa	Wood	63	Yes
4	Tanya	Hide	32	No
5	Arthur	Brain	33	No
6	Willie	Winn	24	No
7	Betty	Wont	64	Yes

The examples in the table on the left refer to this spreadsheet.

Colons are used to show cell ranges. E.g. "A1:D7" would include all the cells in the table above.

The **IF** function confuses people — don't be one of them...

1) The **IF function** gives different results, depending on whether data in other cells matches a condition — e.g. if the number in a cell containing a temperature is negative, the output of the IF function could be "Chilly", while if it's positive, the output could be "Warm".

2) In the above spreadsheet, the percentage scores from a maths exam are in column C. Students with 40% or less haven't passed. The IF function in column D tells the spreadsheet to display the word "No" if the number in column C is 40 or less, and "Yes" if it's above 40.

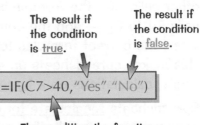

The result if the condition is true.

The result if the condition is false.

=IF(C7>40,"Yes","No")

The condition the function checks (if C7 is greater than 40).

The LOOKUP Function Displays Specified Data

1) The **LOOKUP function** displays data from a table in another part of the spreadsheet.

2) Here, a shop selling vampire supplies has listed its products at the bottom of the spreadsheet. A user enters a product code into cell B1 — the **LOOKUP function** automatically displays the product name in B2 and the price in B3.

3) The formulas in cells B2 and B3 are pretty scary — but basically they search the data in cells **A6-A12**, and display the data in the same row as the relevant product code.

Enter a product code here...

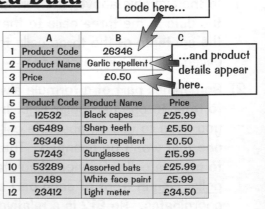

	A	B	C
1	Product Code	26346	
2	Product Name	Garlic repellent	
3	Price	£0.50	
4			
5	Product Code	Product Name	Price
6	12532	Black capes	£25.99
7	65489	Sharp teeth	£5.50
8	26346	Garlic repellent	£0.50
9	57243	Sunglasses	£15.99
10	53289	Assorted bats	£25.99
11	12489	White face paint	£5.99
12	23412	Light meter	£34.50

...and product details appear here.

Where the function looks for the value (the product code column).

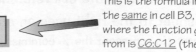

=LOOKUP(B1,A6:A12,B6:B12)

The value the function looks for (the product code).

Where the function gets its result from (the product name column).

This is the formula in cell B2 — it's the same in cell B3, but the column where the function gets its result from is C6:C12 (the price column).

=IF(GCSEGrade>C,"Cheer","Cry")

That was a lot of information, but when you break it all down it's not that bad — even the **IF** and **LOOKUP** functions. You'll need to know how to write each of these functions, so get learning...

Spreadsheets — Charts and Graphs

Graphs and charts are quite similar really — they're just ways of <u>communicating data</u> visually.

Creating a Chart is Dead Easy...

All modern spreadsheets can produce <u>graphs</u> and <u>charts</u> — but each one uses a slightly different method. The basic idea is always the same though.

STEP ONE: Get all the data you want to put into a graph into a <u>single block</u>. It's best if the data is arranged in <u>columns</u>.

STEP TWO: <u>Highlight</u> the data you want to use — you might need to highlight the <u>column headings</u> as well.

STEP THREE: Select the <u>type</u> of chart you want — be sensible and make sure it's <u>suitable</u>.

STEP FOUR: Choose a meaningful <u>title</u> for the chart — one that summarises the contents of the chart, and <u>label</u> any axes.

STEP FIVE: Decide whether the chart needs a <u>key</u> (also called a <u>legend</u>).

	A	B
1	Category	Monthly Spend
2	Food	£7.50
3	Magazines	£1.00
4	CDs	£2.00
5	Going out	£4.00
6	Revision Guides	£6.00

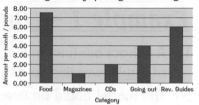

...but you need to know which ones are Appropriate

Spreadsheets can create so many different types of graph — but you need to choose the right kind. Sometimes it's just a matter of <u>taste</u>, but sometimes there are definite <u>rights</u> and <u>wrongs</u>.

1) **BAR GRAPHS** display a <u>category</u> on the x-axis and a <u>value</u> on the y-axis. Use a bar graph when each category is <u>discrete</u> (i.e. separate from the others) — e.g. the number of people who take certain shoe sizes.

2) **LINE GRAPHS** are similar, but are used when the data on the x-axis <u>isn't</u> in categories — like 'time' when you show the temperature of a room over a 24-hour period.

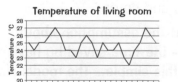

3) **SCATTER GRAPHS** show the <u>relationship</u> between <u>two sets</u> of data — plot one set along the x-axis and one set on the y-axis, and add a <u>trend line</u> to show the relationship more clearly.

4) **PIE CHARTS** show the <u>contributions</u> of categories to a <u>total</u> — e.g. a chart showing what I spend my money on.

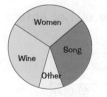

...the size of the cow's udder representing anticipated profits...

It's tempting to try to be too clever, and use <u>fancy</u> graphs that aren't really any clearer than something <u>basic</u>. Again the golden rule is keep it simple — make sure the graph gets its <u>point</u> across, and if possible <u>test</u> your graph by showing it to an intended user.

Pie-charts — I'd prefer pizza-charts myself...

This page is really just <u>basic maths</u>. Learn the page then write out the <u>five steps</u> as a <u>flow chart</u>. Next make a <u>table</u> with headings for <u>type of chart</u>, <u>what it is</u> and <u>when to use it</u> — then <u>fill it in</u>.

Spreadsheets — Modelling

You could get asked about any kind of model or simulation in the exam. But, boring as they are, spreadsheets come up more often than the others. You have been warned.

Three Reasons why Spreadsheets make Good Models

1) Spreadsheets use <u>formulas</u> to try to describe the rules that a real-world phenomenon seems to follow. <u>Input values</u> can then be processed using these formulas to produce <u>output values</u>.

2) Spreadsheets can be used to carry out a <u>what-if analysis</u>. This is when the user changes input values to see the <u>effect</u> on the output of the model. So companies can ask a question like, "What would be the effect on profits if I invested this much money on new machinery?"

3) The output can be in the form of <u>graphs</u> and <u>charts</u> to make the predictions of the model easier to understand.

Example 1 — Queues in a School Canteen

1) A school canteen manager could build a model to represent the relationship between the number of <u>pupils</u> wanting to eat in the canteen, the number of <u>staff</u> and the <u>queuing time</u>.

2) The model could be used to find out the number of staff needed to keep waiting times to a <u>minimum</u>. Taking this one step further, it could be used to find out the <u>minimum number</u> of staff needed to serve all meals in less than an <u>hour</u>.

3) The formula in cell B5 is $=B1*(B3/60)/B2$.
The total time needed for <u>one</u> person to serve all the pupils is equal to the <u>number of pupils</u> (in cell B1) multiplied by the <u>time taken</u> to serve each pupil (in cell B3, divided by 60 to make it minutes). This is then divided by the <u>number of staff</u> to find how long it takes for everyone to be served, using four people. It's assumed that two people can serve meals twice as quickly as one person, three people can serve three times as quickly, and so on.

	A	B
1	Number of pupils	600
2	Number of staff	4
3	Average time to serve a meal (seconds)	20
4		
5	Total serving time (minutes)	50

$=B1*(B3/60)/B2$

Wait while I work out if I need anyone to help me.

4) A <u>weakness</u> of the model is that the assumption about serving times is questionable — the time saved by having extra serving staff may not be this simple. The model also assumes that serving staff can be added forever — but having 100 serving staff would create obvious problems.

Example 2 — Profitable Pizzas

1) A pizza business could build a <u>model</u> to show its profit from selling pizzas. The owner enters data into cells B1 to B4, then the model <u>calculates</u> the data in cells B5 to B7.

2) The firm could then <u>change</u> any of these variables to see the impact of these changes on its profit — e.g. the effect a reduction in sales to 400 and an increase in production costs of 50p per pizza would have on profits.

3) This could be extended to give a direct link between the price of pizzas and the number sold.

	A	B
1	Production cost per pizza	£2.00
2	Other business costs	£1,000
3	Selling price per pizza	£6.00
4	Number of pizzas sold	500
5	Total costs	£2,000
6	Total profit	£1,000
7	Profit per pizza	£2.00

$=B2+(B1*B4)$
$=(B3*B4)-B5$
$=B6/B4$

Simulating canteen queues? It's a pizza cake...

Spreadsheets are quite <u>useful</u> — once you've got your head round how they work. And that's the tricky bit. If you're still struggling with them, go back over the first few pages of this section.

Databases — The Basics

Databases are base-ically (ha ha ha) stacks of <u>fun</u>. I think you'll enjoy the next few pages...

A Database is a Store of Data

1) Databases are used to <u>store</u> lots of data in an <u>organised</u> way.

2) Databases hold data in one or more <u>tables</u>.

3) Each table is organised into <u>fields</u> (columns) and <u>records</u> (rows). Column headings are called <u>field names</u>.

In this table, each column is a different field...   Field name   Primary key

... and each row is a record.

Item of data

First Name	Last Name	Department	Payroll Number	Date of Birth	Salary
Doug	Witherspoon	Catering	100345	26/09/64	£19,000
Neil	Beforem	Customer Service	100346	12/08/76	£15,000
Anita	Dear	Marketing	100347	23/05/83	£18,000
Phil	Ordabuk	Sales	100348	30/03/77	£17,000
Bill	O'Verdue	Finance	100349	22/05/79	£15,000
Stan	D'Alday	Porter	100350	06/11/80	£8,000

4) Each table has a <u>primary key</u>. It's a field which can <u>uniquely</u> identify any record in the table. There can only be <u>one</u> primary key per database table. In the table above, the primary key is the <u>payroll number</u> field — no two people have the same payroll number.

5) The big benefit of databases is that you can <u>search</u> them quickly to find specific data, or use them to generate <u>reports</u> — e.g. which books in a publisher's database have sold the most.

Databases can be Flat-File or Relational

FLAT-FILE DATABASES

1) All the data's organised into <u>one table</u>, which can be viewed by opening <u>one data file</u>.

2) Flat-file databases can be created using <u>all</u> database programs and <u>most</u> spreadsheets.

Name	Relationship Duration	Marks out of 10	Best Feature	Worst Feature
Tracy	3 months	4	Personality	Likes Coldplay
Penny	1 week	6.5	Nostrils	Wears odd socks
Charlie	3 days	7	Legs	Moody
Laura	2 years	1	Her sister	Herself
Rebecca	45 seconds	10	Everything	Lack of commitment

Andy's relational database is updated every time he's dumped.

RELATIONAL DATABASES

1) <u>Relational</u> databases store the data in <u>separate</u> tables.

2) All the data's linked together by <u>key fields</u>.

3) Linking tables together means that important information, such as customer addresses, only needs to be <u>stored once</u> in the database — this <u>reduces data redundancy</u>.

4) It also makes it quick and easy to <u>update</u> information if some of it is wrong — it'll only need changing in one table.

Well-Structured Fields are Really Important

1) The first step in creating a database is to decide on what <u>fields</u> you need. And once you've decided that, each field needs a <u>name</u>, a <u>data type</u> and a <u>format</u>.

2) The <u>data type</u> is dead important, as different <u>processes</u> can be performed on different types of data. The most common data types are in the box — most programs allow others, e.g. <u>pictures</u>, <u>audio</u> and <u>video</u>.

TEXT e.g. Banana
NUMBER e.g. 20 (INTEGER) or 24.41 (REAL)
DATE e.g. 26-09-82 or 26/09/82
TIME e.g. 10:04
CURRENCY e.g. £50.00 or $34.69
BOOLEAN e.g. true or false

Boolean means there are only two possible values — e.g. yes or no, on or off, 1 or 0, etc.

Cow, sheep and wheat — seldom seen data types...

So now you should know the base-ics (I've done it again, I am brilliant) of <u>databases</u>. If you don't, please return to the top of the page and <u>start again</u>. Repeat this process until you know it all...

Databases — Entering Data

Before you enter data, you need to <u>design</u> the <u>table</u> that it's going to live in. Here's how to do it.

A new Database starts with a Table

1) Databases usually have a <u>design view</u>. This is where you set up your table.

2) The design view lets you <u>create</u> fields, <u>name</u> them, give them a <u>data type</u> and set the <u>primary key</u> — you <u>can't</u> input any data in this view.

3) You can also set up <u>data validation rules</u> in the design view. They help to <u>reduce mistakes</u> when data is being entered:

List	This only allows data from a <u>list</u> of options to be entered.
Range check	If the data falls <u>outside</u> of a certain range, e.g. between the years 1900 and 2010, then it <u>can't</u> be entered.
Input mask	This forces data to be entered in a <u>certain format</u>, e.g. DD/MM/YYYY for dates.

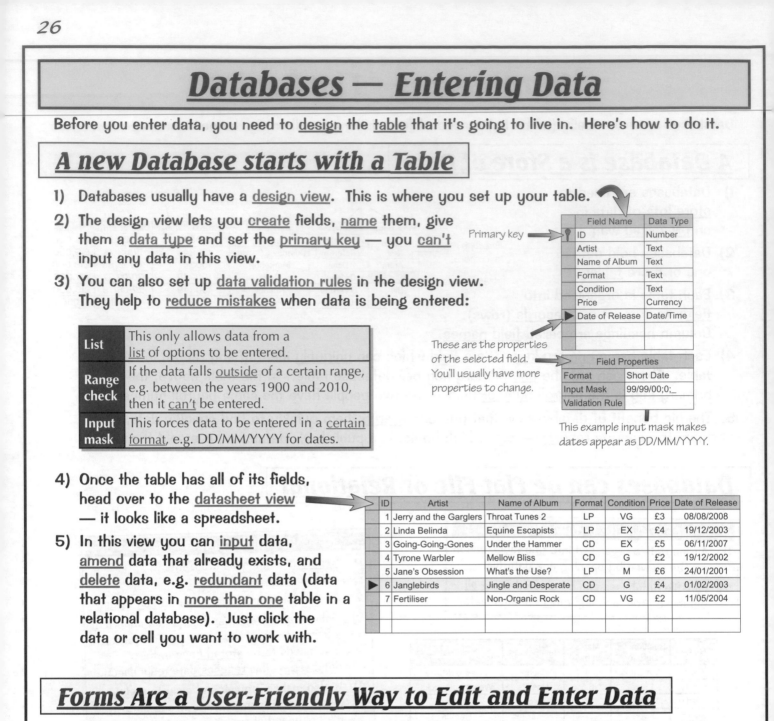

Primary key

Field Name	Data Type
ID	Number
Artist	Text
Name of Album	Text
Format	Text
Condition	Text
Price	Currency
Date of Release	Date/Time

These are the properties of the selected field. You'll usually have more properties to change.

Field Properties	
Format	Short Date
Input Mask	99/99/00;0;_
Validation Rule	

This example input mask makes dates appear as DD/MM/YYYY.

4) Once the table has all of its fields, head over to the <u>datasheet view</u> — it looks like a spreadsheet.

5) In this view you can <u>input</u> data, <u>amend</u> data that already exists, and <u>delete</u> data, e.g. <u>redundant</u> data (data that appears in <u>more than one</u> table in a relational database). Just click the data or cell you want to work with.

ID	Artist	Name of Album	Format	Condition	Price	Date of Release
1	Jerry and the Garglers	Throat Tunes 2	LP	VG	£3	08/08/2008
2	Linda Belinda	Equine Escapists	LP	EX	£4	19/12/2003
3	Going-Going-Gones	Under the Hammer	CD	EX	£5	06/11/2007
4	Tyrone Warbler	Mellow Bliss	CD	G	£2	19/12/2002
5	Jane's Obsession	What's the Use?	LP	M	£6	24/01/2001
6	Janglebirds	Jingle and Desperate	CD	G	£4	01/02/2003
7	Fertiliser	Non-Organic Rock	CD	VG	£2	11/05/2004

Forms Are a User-Friendly Way to Edit and Enter Data

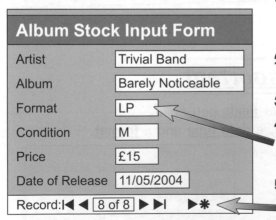

Album Stock Input Form

Artist	Trivial Band
Album	Barely Noticeable
Format	LP
Condition	M
Price	£15
Date of Release	11/05/2004

Record: |◄ ◄ 8 of 8 ► ►| ►✱

1) Forms can be used to <u>enter and edit data</u> in a table. The idea is that they're <u>clearly designed</u> and <u>user-friendly</u> to make this as easy as possible.

2) Forms have to be <u>linked</u> to a table — this tells the form which table's data it should be editing or adding to.

3) Forms also have a <u>design view</u> to adjust their layout.

4) Forms can contain <u>text boxes</u> (for typing into), or <u>tick-boxes</u> and lists for users to choose options from. You can even display <u>input masks</u> in your text boxes.

5) Forms allow users to <u>move</u> through the <u>existing records</u> in a database table and <u>edit</u> them. They also let users create <u>new records</u> in a table.

I'm a confused input form — can you fill me in?

Databases are a bit like a swan. The <u>tables</u> do all the hard work but they're not great looking (like a swan's legs). <u>Forms</u> are the pretty bits that are on show (the bit of a swan above the water).

Databases — Accessing Data

As well as knowing how to create a database you need to know how to <u>interrogate</u> one.

Database Records can be Sorted and Filtered...

1) A <u>sort</u> is the simplest process you can do with a database. You choose a <u>field</u>, and the records are then sorted into order using the <u>entries</u> in that field.

2) Sorts can be done on <u>text fields</u> and <u>numerical fields</u>. With text fields, entries are sorted into alphabetical order.

3) Sorts can either be in <u>ascending</u> order (the lowest value first), or <u>descending</u> order (the highest value first).

> These Fantasy Tiddlywinks League players are sorted in order of transfer value — most valuable first.
>
> | First name | Last name | Team | Value |
> |---|---|---|---|
> | Boris | Batley | Blood and Thunder | £60 |
> | Basher | Best | Workington Warriors | £40 |
> | Freddy | Beech | Joshy's Giants | £15 |
> | Knuckles | Borissov | Higgie's Hairy Men | £5 |
> | Smasher | Bentley | Burton's Brigade | £3.50 |

4) When you're viewing a table, you can apply a <u>filter</u> to see only records that match certain conditions (e.g. players with a value of £60). You can use more than one filter at once.

5) One filtering method is to show records that do or don't match the currently <u>selected</u> data item. You can also filter records by <u>selecting</u> a number of criteria to look for.

6) To view all the records in a table again, just turn the filter <u>off</u>.

...Or Searched

1) Another way to <u>search</u> a database is to use a <u>query</u>. A query is basically a <u>list</u> of the things you want the database to look for.

2) Query <u>results</u> are displayed as a <u>separate datasheet</u> — the table that was queried (searched) remains unchanged and separate from the results. This is <u>different</u> to how a filter works.

3) <u>Simple queries</u> tell the database to look for records that meet just <u>one</u> condition.

Operator	Finds values ...	Operator	Finds values...
=	equal to	<>	not equal to
<	less than	<=	less than or equal to
>	greater than	>=	greater than or equal to

SIMPLE QUERIES
This could be to list all the records of players whose transfer value equals £40 — the query is:
Value = £40.

4) It's also possible to do <u>wildcard searches</u>. These are where you only know <u>part</u> of the value to search for — maybe you can remember that a tiddlywinks player's last name begins with 'Be', but can't remember the <u>full</u> name. You need to use the word '<u>LIKE</u>' together with the <u>*</u> wildcard.

WILDCARD SEARCHES...
Use * to stand for anything. E.g. in Last name LIKE "Be*", the asterisk can stand for anything (or nothing). The results will include Best, Bentley and Beech, but not Batley or Boris.

And if you searched for Team LIKE "*gi*", the results will include Joshy's <u>Gi</u>ants and Hig<u>gi</u>e's Hairy Men.

The * wildcard matches any number of characters. You could also use the ? wildcard — it matches a single character.

COMPLEX SEARCHES...
These search for data meeting more than one condition. You might need to find all the tiddlywinks players called either Boris or Beryl. So your search criteria would be:
First name = "Boris" OR First name = "Beryl"

Or maybe you need to find players called Boris who also have a transfer value over £50. In this case the search is: First name = "Boris" AND Value > £50

Or maybe you're looking for people <u>not</u> called Boris whose transfer value is <u>not</u> over £20. You could use: NOT (First name = "Boris") AND Value <= £20

5) You can also do <u>complex searches</u> — these are when you use <u>AND</u>, <u>OR</u> and <u>NOT</u> to find records that meet more than one condition.

How do I find out about myself? Search me...
You can use the results of a database query to create <u>mail-merged letters</u> (see page 34). Make sure you know all the different ways to access data, including <u>filters</u> and types of <u>queries</u>.

Databases — Reports

A report is the <u>result</u> of a database <u>query</u> that is intended to be seen by someone else. They can either be <u>screen-based</u> or <u>printed</u> depending on what the user needs.

Reports can be in Record or Column Format

1) <u>Record-format</u> reports display each record of data completely separately. They're useful if you want to view each record on its own.

This record format report has been designed to be used as a reminder slip to send to customers whose payments are overdue.

Mortgage Payment Reminder Notice

Name and Postal Address	Account No.
Yoda Murky Swamp District Dagobah System MS5 6RP	07293

Date of Issue:	Amount due
23 June 01	26p

We have still not received payment of the amount shown above.
Please pay this bill immediately.
If you are having difficulty paying, call us on 1236329012.
Your hut may be at risk if you do not keep up with payments.
Offer subject to status. Terms and conditions apply. May the force be with you.

Most database software lets you specify which fields will be displayed in the report.

You can <u>format</u> reports by using different font sizes, colours, headers and footers, and so on. If the database format options are limited, you could <u>export</u> the data into a word processor or desktop publishing package where you have more options.

Account No.	First Name	Date of Issue	Amount Due
07293	Yoda	23 June 01	26p
26438	Darth	4 May 01	13p
14472	Luke	23 April 01	68p
91772	Han	5 June 01	84p

2) <u>Column-format</u> reports display the data in a big <u>table</u>, with <u>all</u> the information shown underneath the field headings. This is more useful if you're interested in comparing values in particular fields across <u>different</u> records.

Reports can be Really Snazzy

1) You can use <u>calculations</u> in your report. For example, a publisher might use a database to store details about the <u>weekly sales</u> of books, with each week's sales in a separate field. The database could then add together the weekly sales for each book and display this on a report as <u>total sales</u>.

2) You can also use charts and graphs in reports. Just select the <u>fields</u> you want to display, select the chart <u>type</u>, give it a <u>title</u> and Bob's your uncle.

Month	Chocolate teapot sales	Motorbike ashtray sales	Waterproof teabag sales
January	15 000	12 000	16 000
February	20 000	17 000	21 000
March	8 000	5 000	9 000
April	10 000	7 000	11 000
May	6 000	3 000	7 000
June	10 000	7 000	11 000
July	30 000	27 000	31 000
August	28 000	25 000	29 000
September	30 000	27 000	31 000
October	13 000	10 000	14 000
November	14 000	11 000	15 000
December	6 000	3 000	7 000

MONEYBAGS INC.
Annual Report

Product	Sales
Chocolate teapot	190 000
Motorbike ashtray	154 000
Waterproof teabag	202 000

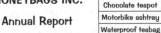

Boring

Just one final note on reports. If you've got a database with lots of tables, you can use <u>any</u> of the data from <u>any</u> table in a <u>single</u> report. At the same time, you can use the data in a <u>single</u> table to produce <u>lots</u> of different reports. Report creation tools in database software are as <u>flexible</u> as a rubber gymnast in a sauna.

<u>Amazing</u>

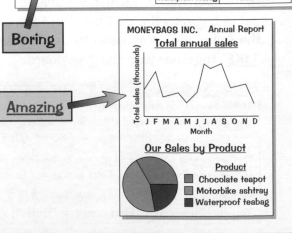

MONEYBAGS INC. Annual Report
Total annual sales

Our Sales by Product

Product
- Chocolate teapot
- Motorbike ashtray
- Waterproof teabag

Reports suggest that students are bored of databases...

This stuff's not difficult — you've just got to remember all the ways you can use the <u>reporting tools</u> in database software. Don't tell anyone, but there's something <u>really</u> good on the next page...

Revision Summary for Section Three

Well done! You've discovered the secret page at the end of Section Three. Quite possibly no other book has this special page. On it you can find the secret to one of life's great mysteries — how to get spreadsheet and database questions right. All you've got to do is answer every one of these little gems — then check and see if you were right. If you get any wrong — just do them again.

1) What is the smallest part of a spreadsheet called?
   a) Sell   b) Smell   c) Cell

2) Which row is cell G14 in?

3) What is a text string?

4) How many different items of data should be entered into a single cell?

5) Name two ways that you can enter data into a cell.

6) What feature of spreadsheet software can be used to edit a cell's contents?

7) Explain fully what conditional formatting is.

8) Describe three other ways to format the data in a spreadsheet.

	A	B
1	Cow	Selling price
2	Daisy	£48.26
3	Buttercup	£58.69
4	Boris	£2.50
5	Total income	

9) What does "absolute cell reference" mean?

10) What function will Farmer Kevin put into cell B5?

11) What does the function =IF(C2>15000,"No pay rise","Pay rise") mean?

12) What does the LOOKUP function do?

13) Explain the difference between a bar graph and a line graph.

14) Explain the difference between a scatter graph and a pie chart.

15) Dodgy Dave wants to use a spreadsheet to help him model the profits from his second-hand balloon business. Give one way he could do this.

16) What is what-if analysis? How could it be used to help model the effects of an increase in patients on waiting times at a doctor's surgery?

17) What is a database? What is a primary key?

18) What might be the primary key in a database listing information about different books?

19) Explain the difference between a flat-file database and a relational database.

20) Name three data types that can be given to a database field.

21) What's the main difference between the design view and datasheet view of a database table?

22) Describe two types of data validation rules.

23) What are database forms used for? Describe two characteristics of a form.

24) Who will appear at the top of a list sorted in descending order of Last Name: Alice Zybrynski or Zack Alphonsus?

25) How are queries and filters different?

26) What's the difference between > and <>?

27) What is a wildcard search? How could one be used to search for all people whose last name begins McD?

28) What are AND, OR and NOT used for?

29) What are the two main ways of setting out a report? How are they different?

30) Describe one way that you can make a database report snazzier.

Word Processing and DTP — Uses

I've shortened Desktop Publishing to <u>DTP</u> — if you worked this out, your <u>prize</u> is a page of revision...

Word Processors and DTP Software are Different

Here are some loose <u>definitions</u> of a word processor and DTP software:

> A <u>word processor</u> allows users to write, edit and format <u>text documents</u>.

> <u>DTP software</u> allows users to create publications that contain <u>text</u> and <u>images</u>.

As <u>technology</u> has advanced, word processors have become able to deal with <u>images</u>, in similar ways to DTP software. However, there's still one major <u>difference</u> between most word processors and DTP software...

DTP Software is usually Frame-Based

1) Frame-based software means that information is put on pages in <u>blocks</u> (called <u>frames</u>).

2) Frames can be <u>moved</u> or <u>resized</u>. This means that it is very easy to <u>edit</u> a DTP document by moving pictures or blocks of text around. Frames can also be moved from page to page.

3) DTP works rather like creating a <u>noticeboard</u> — you have a set of different pieces of information which you can move around until you're happy with the overall layout.

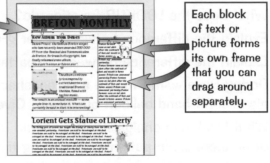

Each block of text or picture forms its own frame that you can drag around separately.

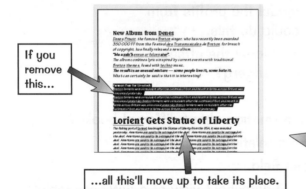

If you remove this...

...all this'll move up to take its place.

4) Most word processors are <u>not</u> frame-based, so the position of one thing depends on the position of everything else. That means moving one thing might make a whole load of other stuff move as well. This doesn't happen with DTP.

(cos it's ace)

Some Uses of Word Processors and DTP Software...

You'd use a <u>word processor</u> to make...

| letters |
| essays |
| memos |
| reports |

These are the uses that the software was designed for — you can make a poster using a word processor, but it's easier to make it with DTP software.

You'd use <u>DTP software</u> to make...

posters	catalogues
leaflets	magazines
flyers	newspapers
brochures	business cards

...documents that are mainly <u>text</u>.

...documents that contain <u>images</u> and <u>text</u>, and that need a <u>flexible layout</u>.

Get yourself in the right frame of mind...

Loads of people think they're <u>experts</u> at using this software — but exam questions are often <u>answered badly</u>. That's because they don't know the <u>basic facts</u> — so get learning. <u>No excuses</u>.

Text Formatting

As well as the <u>common features</u> mentioned on page 16, you can format text in the following ways...

Lists Help to Structure Text

1) <u>Lists</u> are useful for text that can be <u>split up</u> into steps or parts — it makes it easier to read. There are <u>two</u> main types of list:

2) You can also <u>format</u> lists, e.g. use <u>different</u> bullet symbols, <u>letters</u> instead of numbers, <u>full stops</u> not brackets, etc.

3) Most word processors and DTP software can handle <u>sub-numbering</u> — it lets you add <u>more levels</u> to a main point. Here's an example:

> 1) <u>Numbered lists</u>...
> 2) ...where each point...
> 3) ...has a <u>number</u>.

> • <u>Bulleted lists</u>...
> • ...where each point...
> • ...has a <u>bullet symbol</u>.

> 1) This is the first point that I want to mention.
>   i) This point is related to point 1).
>   ii) As is this point.
> 2) This is the next main point that I want to make.

4) The different levels usually have <u>different</u> <u>characters</u> — here, the sub-numbering is done in Roman numerals. (The same kind of thing can also be done on a <u>bulleted list</u>.)

Indents and Tabs set Positions for Text

If you've used a word processor or DTP software, you might have noticed a <u>ruler</u> near the top of the screen. Sometimes the ruler has got <u>weird shapes</u> on it — these are <u>indents</u> and <u>tabs</u>.

<u>Indents</u> determine how close to the edge of the page the text can go (or in DTP software, how close to the edges of the text's <u>frame</u>).

> This line has a left indent of 0 mm.
> This line has a left indent of 10 mm.
> This line has a right indent of 10 mm.

> Tab at 25 mm   Tab at 50 mm
> Some text   More text   Even more text
> Some text   More text   Even more text

<u>Tabs</u> are <u>stops</u> along the ruler that text can be moved to by pressing the <u>Tab key</u> (usually above Caps Lock). They're used to <u>line up</u> bits of text vertically.

Page and Line Breaks Split Up Text

<u>Page</u> and <u>line breaks</u> are just where a <u>new</u> page or line starts. They're usually put in <u>automatically</u>, when a line or page is full. You can also add them <u>manually</u> to help break up big blocks of text.

...<u>easy peasy</u>.

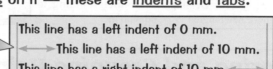

Chapter 1
Chapter 2
Page break
Chapter 1

Line break
Chapter 2

Text Wrap Feeds Text Around Images and Objects

Most software allows you to set how the text wraps — in this example, the text 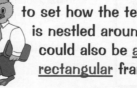 is nestled around the <u>shape</u> of the <u>office duck</u>, but it could also be <u>above</u> and <u>below</u> him or wrapped around his <u>rectangular</u> frame.

> Text wrap can also be called auto wrap — they're the same things though.

Barkeep, a pint of your finest ale — put it on the tab...

Another page of things to learn... who'd have thought it? Thankfully it's nothing too overwhelming, so just <u>knuckle down</u> and get all of these <u>formatting features</u> stashed away in your memory box.

Improving Presentation

Now you know how to format text, here a few tricks to make documents look a bit snazzier.

Tables, Borders and Columns can Help Readability

1) Tables are a good way to present lists of numerical or text information, e.g. lists of names and addresses.

2) Most word processors and DTP software will let you create tables from scratch. And when you paste in data from a spreadsheet it's often formatted into a table (although only the values will be carried across — things like formulas will be lost).

3) Just like with spreadsheets, you can merge the cells in a table (see page 20). If you change your mind, you can split them up into single cells again. Phew.

4) Amazingly, you can format the different parts of a table — border thickness and colour, cell fill colour, vertical alignment, etc. can all be adjusted to suit the document.

Ralph found that the best way to present himself was by using a table.

Wordprocessing Weekly News

Typists around the country were staggered to learn yesterday that text can be arranged automatically in columns.

"I'm staggered," said 38-year-old Ian Denting. "If these newfangled word processors keep going at this rate then I'm going to become marginalised."

Nelson Column, of London, said it had "absolutely nothing to do with me."

5) Putting borders around tables, pictures, whole pages or blocks of text helps break up the information on the page — which sometimes makes it easier to read. Or you might just want to make things look nice and pretty...

6) Columns can be created so that the text flows down the page and jumps automatically to the next column. This is great for newsletters and newspapers.

Layering and Grouping Help When Creating Documents

1) Most word processors and DTP software let you stack things on top of each other.

2) Adjusting the stacking order changes how these things overlap.

3) Layering takes the idea of stacking one step further. Layers are like separate transparent sheets, which you can create different parts of a page on. The layers are then stacked on top of each other.

4) You can adjust the stacking order of layers, and you can also turn them on and off — this makes it easy to hide parts of a document.

5) Grouping means a number of separate items are treated as one thing.

6) The good thing about grouping is that it's not permanent. You can ungroup objects and they'll be treated as separate things again.

A thrilling example of stacking in action.

Grouping is useful for keeping items together if you move things around a lot.

Watermarks draw Attention to the Page

A watermark is an image or text that appears behind the main text in a document. For example:

To let people know the status of the document, e.g. 'draft' or 'top secret'.

To make documents look nicer, e.g. to make a love letter even more sickly sweet than it already was.

Adjust the stacking order of your hair for a layered look...

I hope you're still awake, there are a few more pages to go. The key to all these features is using them wisely — tables may improve readability, but don't go crazy and put everything in one.

Advanced Features

Some <u>more features</u> for you to learn about. Although it says 'advanced', it's <u>not</u> really that difficult.

Headings and Subheadings Break Text into Logical Chunks

1) A <u>heading</u> describes the <u>main topic</u> — this page's heading is 'Advanced Features'.
<u>Subheadings</u> are <u>separate</u> topics that are part of the main topic — the yellow boxes on this page.

2) You can assign <u>styles</u> to headings and subheadings.
A style is a <u>set</u> of <u>formatting options</u> that can be applied to text.
Styles are <u>useful</u> for two main reasons:

   - They help give documents a <u>consistent appearance</u>, which makes documents look more <u>professional</u>.
   - They let you <u>change</u> the <u>look</u> of a whole document really <u>easily</u> — you just update the <u>styles</u> instead of every single piece of text in the document.

   <u>Style sheets</u> contain information about all the different styles used in a document.

3) Word processors and DTP software can also use styles to generate a <u>table of contents</u> — you tell it what styles to include, and it sorts everything out <u>automatically</u>.

Sections Split Documents into Parts

1) You can split a document up into <u>sections</u>.

2) This creates different parts that can have their <u>own page numbering</u> — e.g. one could have Roman numerals (i, ii, iii...), while another could have letters (a, b, c...).

3) Different sections could also have their own <u>headers and footers</u>.

A fancy word for the numbering of pages is pagination — word processors and DTP software let you fiddle with pagination to your heart's content.

Mind Your Language with Spelling and Grammar Checkers

<u>Grammar</u> and <u>spelling</u> checkers should improve your written communication — but there are potential <u>problems</u>.

<u>GRAMMAR CHECKERS:</u>
Grammar-checkers can be <u>unreliable</u> and give confusing advice. This is because good grammar depends upon <u>context</u> — and most software isn't yet powerful enough to take this into account.

<u>SPELLING CHECKERS:</u>

1) They come in different <u>languages</u>. Many words are spelt differently in different parts of the English speaking world — e.g. labor (American English) and labour (UK English). So if you live in the UK, check that you're using <u>UK English</u>.

2) They only recognise misspelt words — not their <u>context</u>. This is a problem with words like 'were' and 'where'. If you use the wrong one, the spell-checker won't find a problem.

3) Sometimes the dictionaries contain <u>mistakes</u>. A version of one well-known word processor's spell-checker contained a <u>misspelling</u> of 'liaise'.

Check the Word Count

1) Sometimes you need to know <u>how many</u> words you've written, e.g. in a piece of coursework.

2) Automatic <u>word counting</u> is an option in most word processors and DTP software.

I done a grammer and spellin cheque on this page...

I can reliably inform you that there are <u>462 words</u> on this page. Every single one is <u>important</u>, so get your learning hat on and go over the page until you know these <u>advanced features</u> inside out.

Mail Merge

Mail merge lets you <u>merge</u> data from a <u>data source</u> (e.g. <u>spreadsheet</u> or <u>database</u>) into a word processor or a DTP document. This is <u>incredibly</u> useful if you need to send out stacks and stacks of <u>standard documents</u> with just a few details (like the name and address) changed each time.

First, You'll Need Some Data to Merge...

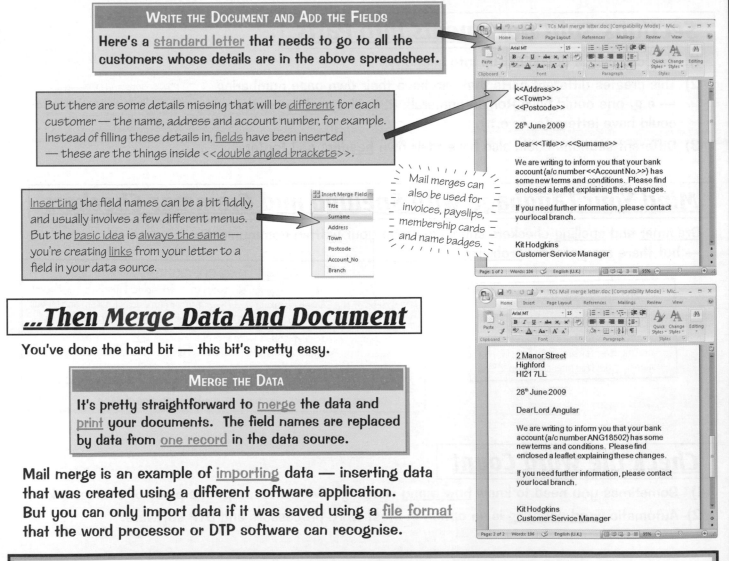

ORGANISE YOUR DATA

You'll need the source of the <u>data</u> that you want to merge into your document. Here, the data's in a <u>spreadsheet</u>.

The first row shows the names of the <u>data fields</u>. Other rows each contain one complete <u>record</u> (see page 25 for a definition).

...Then You Need a Document, Complete with Merge Fields...

WRITE THE DOCUMENT AND ADD THE FIELDS

Here's a <u>standard letter</u> that needs to go to all the customers whose details are in the above spreadsheet.

But there are some details missing that will be <u>different</u> for each customer — the name, address and account number, for example. Instead of filling these details in, <u>fields</u> have been inserted — these are the things inside <<<u>double angled brackets</u>>>.

<u>Inserting</u> the field names can be a bit fiddly, and usually involves a few different menus. But the <u>basic idea</u> is <u>always the same</u> — you're creating <u>links</u> from your letter to a field in your data source.

Mail merges can also be used for invoices, payslips, membership cards and name badges.

...Then Merge Data And Document

You've done the hard bit — this bit's pretty easy.

MERGE THE DATA

It's pretty straightforward to <u>merge</u> the data and <u>print</u> your documents. The field names are replaced by data from <u>one record</u> in the data source.

Mail merge is an example of <u>importing</u> data — inserting data that was created using a different software application. But you can only import data if it was saved using a <u>file format</u> that the word processor or DTP software can recognise.

Congratulations, «Title» «Surname»! You've won!

Mail merge looks more fiddly than it is — the key is <u>practice</u>. So on your birthday, why not use mail merge to write standard thank you letters to your friends and relatives. They'll be <u>impressed</u>...

Revision Summary for Section Four

Another section down, another set of questions to test just how much knowledge you have gained. The usual terms and conditions apply — have a go at these questions and if you get any wrong, head back to the page in question and learn it all again until your brain is swollen with information.

1) Describe the main difference between word processors and DTP software.

2) Give three uses of word processors.

3) And in a completely unexpected move, give three uses of DTP software.

4) Name the two main types of lists.

5) What is sub-numbering?

6) What do indents determine?

7) What are tabs used for?

8) Give two ways you could break up a big block of text.

9) Name the text formatting feature that lets you nestle text around an image.

10) What might you use to display a long list of names and telephone numbers in a document?

11) Give two ways that borders can improve presentation.

12) What is a layer? What are layers used for?

13) Explain what grouping is.

14) Give two reasons why watermarks are used on some documents.

15) What is a heading? How is a subheading different?

16) In DTP or word processing, what is a style?

17) Describe one reason why styles are useful.

18) Give one reason why a document might be split up into sections.

19) Describe two reasons why spelling checkers aren't completely reliable.

20) What two things do you need before you can carry out a mail merge?

21) What happens when you merge the data in a spreadsheet with merge fields in a letter?

22) Explain what is meant by importing data.

Presentation Software

Presentation software is used to give <u>talks</u> and <u>display</u> ideas. You need to know its <u>main features</u>.

Presentations are Created as a Series of Slides

1) Presentation software creates a series of <u>slides</u> in a single document. Each slide contains a number of <u>frames</u> (a bit like DTP software, see page 30).

2) Each slide usually contains <u>text</u> or <u>images</u> — but you can put <u>movies</u> and <u>sound</u> on slides too.

3) The software makes it easy to <u>insert</u> and <u>delete</u> slides, and to change their <u>order</u>.

4) The really <u>clever</u> thing about presentation software is that you can <u>animate</u> things — e.g. make them move around and flash and spin... and so on.

5) This helps to <u>capture</u> an audience's <u>attention</u> and can help <u>presenters</u> make their <u>points</u>.

Animations and Transitions bring Slides to Life

1) <u>Animations</u> make the <u>frames</u> on a slide arrive on screen in different ways. For example...

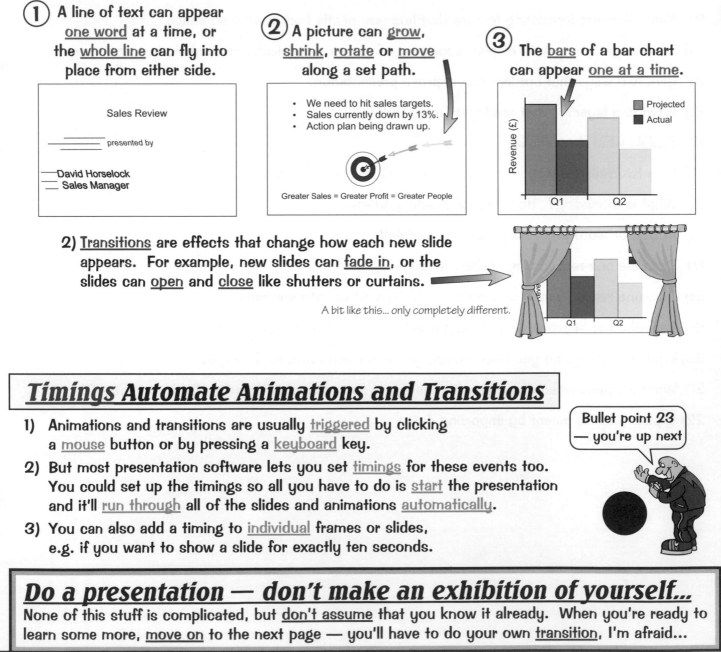

① A line of text can appear <u>one word</u> at a time, or the <u>whole line</u> can fly into place from either side.

Sales Review

_____ presented by

David Horselock
Sales Manager

② A picture can <u>grow</u>, <u>shrink</u>, <u>rotate</u> or <u>move</u> along a set path.

- We need to hit sales targets.
- Sales currently down by 13%.
- Action plan being drawn up.

Greater Sales = Greater Profit = Greater People

③ The <u>bars</u> of a bar chart can appear <u>one at a time</u>.

Revenue (£)

Projected
Actual

Q1   Q2

2) <u>Transitions</u> are effects that change how each new slide appears. For example, new slides can <u>fade in</u>, or the slides can <u>open</u> and <u>close</u> like shutters or curtains.

A bit like this... only completely different.

Q1   Q2

Timings Automate Animations and Transitions

1) Animations and transitions are usually <u>triggered</u> by clicking a <u>mouse</u> button or by pressing a <u>keyboard</u> key.

2) But most presentation software lets you set <u>timings</u> for these events too. You could set up the timings so all you have to do is <u>start</u> the presentation and it'll <u>run through</u> all of the slides and animations <u>automatically</u>.

3) You can also add a timing to <u>individual</u> frames or slides, e.g. if you want to show a slide for exactly ten seconds.

Bullet point 23 — you're up next

Do a presentation — don't make an exhibition of yourself...

None of this stuff is complicated, but <u>don't assume</u> that you know it already. When you're ready to learn some more, <u>move on</u> to the next page — you'll have to do your own <u>transition</u>, I'm afraid...

Presentation Software

There are a just few <u>more features</u> in presentation software that you need to know about.... ·

Consistent Colour Schemes and Simple Layouts are Good

1) The most <u>effective</u> and <u>professional-looking</u> slides use a good, <u>consistent colour scheme</u>, and they have a <u>simple layout</u>.

A <u>good</u> colour scheme is a set of colours that <u>look good together</u>.

2) Most presentation software has a selection of ready-made <u>colour schemes</u> to use on your slides. You select a colour scheme, and the software will <u>automatically</u> apply the right colours to slide <u>backgrounds</u> and <u>text</u>.

3) You can usually select a <u>template</u> layout for your slides, e.g. one with just a title and a text frame, one with two columns, a blank one, etc.

See p38 for more about templates.

For Fancy Slides, add Hyperlinks, Buttons and Multimedia

1) <u>Hyperlinks</u> are a way of <u>moving around</u> a presentation (instead of just moving through all the slides in the planned order). They're useful if you want to jump to a particular slide, e.g. to refer to some figures on the last slide or to view the first slide again.

2) Hyperlinks are <u>attached</u> to objects, e.g. some text or a picture — you just <u>click</u> the hyperlink to be taken to the destination slide.

3) Some hyperlinks look like <u>animated buttons</u> that seem like they're being pushed in when you click them.

4) Most presentation software even lets you add <u>multimedia clips</u> to presentations, e.g. <u>video clips</u> and <u>sound effects</u>.

5) You can change:
- <u>when</u> the clips start (e.g. when the first slide appears or when the presenter clicks a button),
- how loud the <u>volume</u> is,
- whether the clip <u>starts again</u> once it reaches the end, or just <u>stops</u>.

My Brilliant Holiday

What do you mean, 'they came here for a talk on e-commerce'?

Presentations can be Viewed On-Screen and on Paper

Slide 1	
Slide 2	
Slide 3	

Notes

Slide 1	Slide 2
Slide 3	Slide 4
Slide 5	Slide 6

1) You can view your presentations on a <u>monitor</u> — but for large audiences, you might need to <u>project</u> the presentation onto a <u>large screen</u>.

2) You can also print <u>paper handouts</u> of the slides for members of the audience, or for the presenter.
- Each page of the handouts might show <u>more than one</u> slide.
- Handouts can be <u>annotated</u> (show extra notes as well as what's on the slide — e.g. the presenter can add reminders of what to say).

3) Handouts make it easier to <u>follow</u> a presentation, and people can scribble their own <u>notes</u> on the printout too.

Consistency REALLY does make things look nice...

It's quite <u>easy</u> to make a presentation look <u>awful</u> — billions of <u>different</u> animations, transitions and colours just put people off and then the presentation ends up being <u>useless</u>. So be warned...

Web-Design Software

Making a website used to be the preserve of the supergeek — now everyone's at it...

Web Design Software is a Bit Like a Word Processor...

1) For the most part, using web design software is similar to using a word processor (see page 30). You can add text, pictures and so on in much the same way.

2) The end result is a website, made up of individual web pages.

3) The software will also convert your website to HTML, the standard code that web browsers (see page 55) understand.

> HTML stands for HyperText Markup Language — you might not need to know this, but I knew you were wondering what it meant.

4) Here are two features that you'll find in most web design software:

> **Master pages**: these are pages containing objects that need to appear on all pages. They save a lot of effort and they're good for consistency, e.g. so headings are in the same place on each page.

> **Templates**: these are pages that are partially completed — you just amend the headings and change the text etc. for each particular page.

5) The above features give a consistent look to your pages, which makes them look professional.

...with Added Web Features

You can use these things on websites to make them more fancy — otherwise they'll just be like a text document that's been put on the Web, which is boring...

Marquee: this effect makes text scroll across the screen. It does annoy some people though.

RSS Feed: this lets people subscribe to your website, so when you update the content of your webpages the subscribers will be told automatically.

Hyperlinks: these take you from one page to another. They're useful if you've got a lot of pages in your website. They can also link to other people's websites.

Hotspots: these are hyperlinks that are attached to an image. You can create several hotspots on one image, so clicking on different parts of the image takes you to different webpages.

Forms: these capture information from website users, e.g. their name and email address, or feedback.

Animations: these are moving images (see page 41) — some web design software lets you create animations.

Navigation Bars and Counters are Useful Features

1) You could include a navigation bar on your website. It's a menu of hyperlinks that is on each page of a website, to make it easier for users to find what they want. Usually the pages that people want to visit frequently are on the navigation bar, e.g. the homepage or search page.

2) Counters are useful to see how many visitors you've had to your website. Some counters will ignore repeat visitors, so you know how many individuals have visited your website.

Spiders are the masters of web design...

You've probably been on a website before, but you might not have made one. Even if you have, make sure you learn the stuff on this page from top to bottom — it might come up in your exam.

Audio and Video Software

If you want to learn about <u>audio</u> and <u>video software</u>, you've come to the right place. Step right in...

Media Players — You know what they are...

1) You need a <u>media player</u> to <u>watch</u> a video (e.g. a DVD or a video file) or <u>listen</u> to some audio (e.g. a CD or MP3 file).

2) Media players can be a separate piece of <u>hardware</u> (like a DVD player under your telly), or a piece of <u>software</u> installed on your computer. They all have the same <u>basic features</u>.

3) Some have extra features, like the ability to display <u>subtitles</u>.

4) Most software media players also let you create <u>playlists</u>, which are <u>custom lists</u> of media files that the media player will <u>play in order</u>.

- Play/Start
- Stop
- Pause
- Fast forward
- Reverse
- Volume adjustment and mute (i.e. no sound at all)

Creating and Editing Media Files is a bit more Interesting

You'll need a selection of <u>hardware</u> and <u>software</u> to <u>create</u> and <u>edit</u> media files on a computer, e.g:

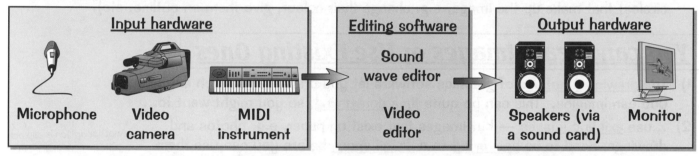

Input hardware

Microphone Video camera MIDI instrument

Editing software

Sound wave editor

Video editor

Output hardware

Speakers (via a sound card) Monitor

MIDI = Musical Instrument Digital Interface. MIDI signals contain data on pitch, volume, intensity etc., but no actual sound.

A musical stave

1) Media can be recorded in <u>analogue</u> or <u>digital</u> formats — but before you can <u>edit</u> an analogue recording on a computer, you'll need to <u>convert</u> it to a digital format. See page 44 for more on this.

2) It's also possible to <u>compose</u> music using software. Some software lets you add notes to an on-screen <u>stave</u> pretty much like you would with a pen and paper — it can then <u>play</u> the piece back to you.

3) <u>Sound-wave editors</u> let you adjust sounds in all kinds of fancy ways (e.g. you can add different effects, change the tempo, and all sorts).

Media Files can be Downloaded or Streamed

1) Media files can be stored on a <u>server</u> (see page 51) — people access these servers through the <u>Internet</u> and can <u>download</u> (save) the media files to their own computer before playing them.

2) <u>Streaming</u> is like downloading, but the media file is <u>played</u> through a media player <u>without</u> being stored on the computer. It's like watching a film on **TV**, rather than on a DVD.

3) Podcasts are a <u>series</u> of media files that are placed on a server as <u>episodes</u>. People can <u>download</u> podcasts at <u>any time</u> and play them in <u>any</u> suitable media player, <u>not</u> just the well known one that the name suggests...

4) Podcasts can be used for <u>loads</u> of things — <u>news reports</u>, <u>comedy shows</u>, <u>educational material</u>... In a nutshell, they're a <u>modern</u> and convenient way of <u>broadcasting</u>.

I thought a pod cast was put on a broken runner bean...

All this technology is probably <u>second-nature</u> for you youngsters, but you've still got to <u>learn it all</u>.
I'm still using a <u>turntable</u> to listen to my favourite <u>waltzes</u> — and one-two-three, one-two-three...

Graphics Software

This page is for all you budding Rembrandts — you'll soon know all about graphics software...

Images are Stored as either Bitmap or Vector Data

BITMAP IMAGES — *made with 'painting' software.*

1) The graphic is saved as a series of coloured dots (pixels) in a file called a bitmap. These files are large — each dot in a red circle would be saved individually.

2) To edit the image, you basically alter each dot, but there are lots of tools to make this easier.

Resolution means the number of pixels making up the image. The more pixels used, the sharper the image — but the bigger the file. If you change the size of the image, the software has to add or remove pixels to fit the new size — this reduces the image quality, making things blurry.

400 pixels / 400 pixels / 50 pixels / 50 pixels

VECTOR IMAGES — *made with 'drawing' software.*

1) The image is saved as coordinates and equations (e.g. a red circle might be represented by its radius, the coordinates of its centre and a number for its colour).

2) Vector images are much easier to edit than bitmap images — you can resize them without reducing image quality and you can manipulate the individual objects (e.g. squares, circles) that make up the image, e.g. change their colour, give them an outline, etc).

You can Create Images or Use Existing Ones

1) The drawing functions of graphics software let you draw pretty much anything you can imagine. This can be quite time consuming, so you might want to...

2) ...use existing images — but images that exist on paper, e.g. photos and drawings, need to be converted to a digital image before you can use them — this is what a scanner does. You can also upload images from a digital camera to your computer, which the software can work with straight away.

Another option is clip art graphics — digital images that have been made by someone else for you to use.

Tools for Creating and Editing Images

Straight lines and freehand lines can be drawn with different properties — thickness or colour can be changed.

Graphics software has tools to draw simple shapes like squares, rectangles, circles, triangles, and so on. You can then edit these basic shapes to make arrows, speech bubbles and other more complex designs.

Fill and shading tools let you change the colours and backgrounds of objects. You can have patterned fills as well as single colours and gradients (transitions from one colour to another).

You can change the size of any object by dragging one of the handles (around the outside of the image) outwards or inwards. But if you don't keep the proportions the same, you can end up with very stretched or squashed images.

It's also possible to construct an image using different objects — the seal originally balanced a ball but that part of the graphic can be removed and replaced with pretty much anything.

Because most vector graphics (except basic shapes) consist of separate objects, it's easy to change the colour of certain parts of the graphic, like this jacket and trousers, by recolouring individual objects.

In painting software, you can freehand draw with a brush or air brush. You can also erase pixels.

Brush / Air brush / Eraser

Learn this page from top to toe and vector-y will be yours...

There are other fancy things that graphics software can do, e.g. make objects transparent, distort them and clone (duplicate) them. But now I think it's time to get animated about your revision...

Animation Software

Not all exam boards expect you to know about animations. But just in case yours does...

Animations are Made Up of Frames

1) Animations are a collection of <u>frames</u> — a frame is basically an <u>individual image</u>.

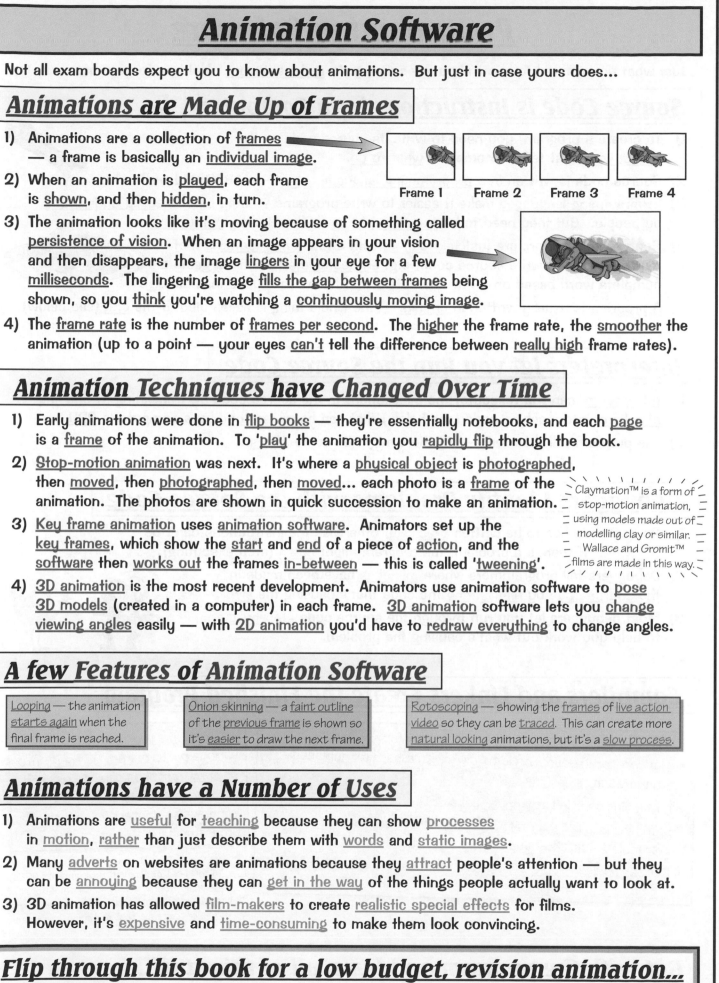

Frame 1   Frame 2   Frame 3   Frame 4

2) When an animation is <u>played</u>, each frame is <u>shown</u>, and then <u>hidden</u>, in turn.

3) The animation looks like it's moving because of something called <u>persistence of vision</u>. When an image appears in your vision and then disappears, the image <u>lingers</u> in your eye for a few <u>milliseconds</u>. The lingering image <u>fills the gap between frames</u> being shown, so you <u>think</u> you're watching a <u>continuously moving image</u>.

4) The <u>frame rate</u> is the number of <u>frames per second</u>. The <u>higher</u> the frame rate, the <u>smoother</u> the animation (up to a point — your eyes <u>can't</u> tell the difference between <u>really high</u> frame rates).

Animation Techniques have Changed Over Time

1) Early animations were done in <u>flip books</u> — they're essentially notebooks, and each <u>page</u> is a <u>frame</u> of the animation. To 'play' the animation you <u>rapidly flip</u> through the book.

2) <u>Stop-motion animation</u> was next. It's where a <u>physical object</u> is <u>photographed</u>, then <u>moved</u>, then <u>photographed</u>, then <u>moved</u>... each photo is a <u>frame</u> of the animation. The photos are shown in quick succession to make an animation.

Claymation™ is a form of stop-motion animation, using models made out of modelling clay or similar. Wallace and Gromit™ films are made in this way.

3) <u>Key frame animation</u> uses <u>animation software</u>. Animators set up the <u>key frames</u>, which show the <u>start</u> and <u>end</u> of a piece of <u>action</u>, and the <u>software</u> then <u>works out</u> the frames <u>in-between</u> — this is called '<u>tweening</u>'.

4) <u>3D animation</u> is the most recent development. Animators use animation software to <u>pose</u> <u>3D models</u> (created in a computer) in each frame. <u>3D animation</u> software lets you <u>change</u> <u>viewing angles</u> easily — with <u>2D animation</u> you'd have to <u>redraw everything</u> to change angles.

A few Features of Animation Software

<u>Looping</u> — the animation <u>starts again</u> when the final frame is reached.

<u>Onion skinning</u> — a <u>faint outline</u> of the <u>previous frame</u> is shown so it's <u>easier</u> to draw the next frame.

<u>Rotoscoping</u> — showing the <u>frames</u> of <u>live action</u> <u>video</u> so they can be <u>traced</u>. This can create more <u>natural looking</u> animations, but it's a <u>slow process</u>.

Animations have a Number of Uses

1) Animations are <u>useful</u> for <u>teaching</u> because they can show <u>processes</u> in <u>motion</u>, <u>rather</u> than just describe them with <u>words</u> and <u>static images</u>.

2) Many <u>adverts</u> on websites are animations because they <u>attract</u> people's attention — but they can be <u>annoying</u> because they can <u>get in the way</u> of the things people actually want to look at.

3) 3D animation has allowed <u>film-makers</u> to create <u>realistic special effects</u> for films. However, it's <u>expensive</u> and <u>time-consuming</u> to make them look convincing.

Flip through this book for a low budget, revision animation...

The best way to start an animation is by making a <u>storyboard</u> — a set of <u>still images</u> that mark out <u>key points</u> in the animation. It'll help you to <u>focus</u> your ideas and make the whole process <u>easier</u>.

Programming Software

Just what you wanted to know about — software to make software. Hold on to your hats...

Source Code is Instructions for a Computer

1) To create a program, you need to write its source code — the instructions that tell the computer what to do.

2) Source code is written in a programming language, e.g. C++, BASIC, Java™, etc.

3) Programming languages make it easier to write programs — they can be easily understood by people. But they need to be translated to be understood by computers.

4) Source-code editors are just text editors with a few fancy features that make it easier to write source code, e.g. autocomplete (which suggests a complete word based on a few characters that have been typed in... handy).

5) A program is usually written in chunks — the whole thing is assembled at the end (see below).

Interpreters let you Run the Source Code

1) Interpreters can run (execute) the instructions in the source code by translating it, one line at a time, into machine code (see below) that can be understood by a computer's CPU.

2) The program will then run — but there might be some errors...

Debuggers Identify Problems with the Source Code

1) Source code has to be written precisely, otherwise the instructions can't be followed. If there's a problem, the program might crash (stop executing).

2) Debuggers tell programmers where mistakes have been made in the source code by highlighting the code that's causing the error.

3) Most debuggers let you run through the source code step-by-step, to help you work out what's causing the problem.

Compilers and Linkers Create the Finished Program

1) A compiler translates high-level (i.e. easy for humans to understand) source code to low-level (i.e. hard for humans to understand) machine code.

2) Machine code is the language of a CPU.

3) Compiling is like interpreting, but all of the source code is translated at the same time, rather than line by line.

4) It can be a slow process, but the final machine code is executed more quickly than if it's interpreted line by line.

A linker joins together (links) the various parts of compiled code into one program that can be executed and understood by a CPU. On Windows computers, executable programs have a .exe extension.

Integrated Development Environments (IDEs) are single programs that contain most or all of the programs mentioned on this page. IDEs make it easier to create, test and compile programs.

Get with the program and learn all of this stuff...

This page might seem complicated, but it's a piece of cake. The basic order is write the source code, debug it, compile it and then link the compiled bits together. Nothing difficult at all.

Revision Summary for Section Five

That section was quite a mixed bag, but hopefully you've not lost your way... because it's time to see just how much you really know. The same rules as always apply — try one of the following questions and if you get it right, give yourself a high five and then move on to the next one. If you get it wrong, make a sad face and then skip back to the page with the answer on — learn all of it again and then come back here for a rematch.

1) Describe one similarity between presentation software and DTP software.

2) Name two ways that presentation slides can be brought to life. Give an example of each.

3) Describe how "timings" could be used to automate a presentation.

4) Describe two features of a professional-looking presentation.

5) Why might you use hyperlinks in a presentation?

6) Name two ways that presentations can be viewed.

7) Describe one feature that's found in both web design software and word processors.

8) What is a hotspot?

9) How can you capture information from users of your website?

10) What is a navigation bar?

11) Give an example of a media player.

12) Name three basic features that are standard to most media players.

13) Describe one piece of software that you could use to create or edit sounds.

14) Describe the difference between streaming and downloading.

15) What is the difference between bitmap and vector images?

16) Describe three tools in graphics software that help you to create and edit images.

17) What is each separate 'picture' in an animation called?

18) Describe the phenomenon of 'persistence of vision'.

19) Describe two animation techniques.

20) Give one advantage and one disadvantage of using 3D animation in a film.

21) What is source code?

22) Name one feature of a source code editor.

23) How does an interpreter run source code?

24) What software features can help to fix problems with source code?

25) Describe the main advantage of compiling source code, rather than interpreting it.

26) What does a linker do?

Data Logging

The stuff in this section is about different ways of <u>recording</u>, <u>responding to</u> and <u>controlling</u> events, either in the real world or in a <u>model</u> of it. Even if you've not had much of a chance to carry out this sort of ICT in your school, learn it — because it's in the exam.

Data Logging means Recording Data Automatically

1) <u>Data logging</u> means <u>capturing</u> information using <u>sensors</u>.

2) Measurements are taken, and then converted to <u>data</u> and <u>stored</u>. They can then be <u>downloaded</u> into a computer for analysis.

3) Data logging is best used whenever <u>large amounts</u> of data need to be collected over very <u>long</u> or <u>short</u> periods of time, or from <u>hostile</u> environments.

4) Examples of data logging activities include collecting weather data via <u>satellite</u>, radioactivity data from <u>nuclear power</u> stations, and temperature data from inside a <u>pizza oven</u>.

Got to test the quality of these pizzas every twenty-three minutes.

Data Logging needs the Right Hardware and Software

1) Data is collected by an <u>input sensor</u>. Most sensors work by converting environmental signals into <u>electrical</u> energy — producing either an <u>analogue</u> or a <u>digital</u> signal.

2) A detector at a set of traffic lights produces a signal whenever a vehicle passes near it. This is a <u>digital</u> sensor — it's either on or off.

3) A thermistor is a resistor whose resistance changes with temperature — the hotter the thermistor, the more easily electricity flows through it. Output from a thermistor can take a range of values — it's an <u>analogue</u> signal.

4) Before an <u>analogue</u> signal can be stored and downloaded onto a computer system, it needs to be converted into a <u>digital</u> signal — using an <u>analogue-to-digital converter</u> (<u>ADC</u>).

SENSORS ARE OFTEN USED TO MEASURE...	
Light:	Light-dependent resistors are used to determine when to switch street lights on.
Radioactivity:	Geiger counters measure the amount of radioactivity emitted by a source.
Temperature:	Thermistors can be used to control an air-conditioning system.
Sound:	Sensors can be used to check that aircraft noise keeps within agreed levels.
Pressure:	Like pressure pads used in burglar alarm systems.
Infrared:	A sensor can detect a break in an infrared beam.
Air pressure:	Sensors can be used to control emergency oxygen masks on aircraft.

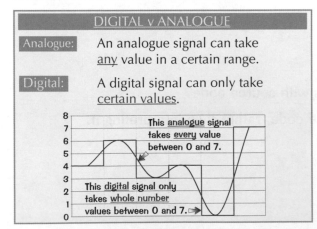

DIGITAL v ANALOGUE	
Analogue:	An analogue signal can take <u>any</u> value in a certain range.
Digital:	A digital signal can only take <u>certain values</u>.

This analogue signal takes every value between 0 and 7.

This digital signal only takes whole number values between 0 and 7.

5) An ADC is often part of the <u>interface board</u> (the device that lets you connect the sensor to the computer).

6) Once the output's been converted into digital data, it's often stored in <u>CSV</u> (comma-separated value) format. This means that it can be <u>imported</u> into a spreadsheet for data analysis. The output from this analysis can be screen-based or paper-based, and will probably include graphs.

Converting analogue to digital, as easy as ADC...

Make sure you learn what data logging is, what hardware and software is needed, the difference between analogue and digital signals, and what sensors can measure. Yep — learn it <u>all</u>.

Logging Period and Interval

This stuff's just <u>common sense</u> — but that doesn't mean you don't have to bother learning it.

Choose an Appropriate Logging Period...

1) The <u>logging period</u> is just the <u>total</u> length of time you're going to collect data for. If this is too long, you can <u>waste</u> valuable time. But if it's too short, you might <u>miss</u> some important data.

2) The logging period <u>depends</u> on the thing that's being <u>monitored</u>. For example, an experiment to investigate the cooling of a cup of coffee should not take measurements over a two-year period — one hour would be better.

3) If you're not sure what logging period to use, do some <u>preliminary research</u> — for example, leave a cup of coffee and see roughly how long it takes.

...and a Logging Interval

1) The <u>logging interval</u> is the time <u>between</u> one measurement and the next.

2) As a general rule, the longer the logging period, the longer the logging interval can be.

USE A LONG LOGGING INTERVAL...	USE A SHORT LOGGING INTERVAL...
If you're measuring the growth of a tree over a two-year period, you could probably have a logging interval of a month.	On the other hand, measuring the temperature of a chemical reaction which lasts only a couple of seconds might require a logging interval of a fraction of a second.

3) Once you've decided on a logging period and logging interval, you can work out the <u>number</u> of <u>readings</u> you'll have — be careful not to make this too <u>small</u>.

$$\text{Number of readings} = \frac{\text{Logging period}}{\text{Logging interval}}$$

Data Logging has Advantages and Disadvantages

ADVANTAGES

1) <u>Data logging</u> can record information in places where <u>humans</u> find it <u>hard</u> to operate — e.g. the bottom of the sea, outer space, and inside nuclear reactors or pizza ovens.

2) Data can be collected over very <u>long</u> or very <u>short</u> periods — you could record the growth rate of a tree, or the <u>rapidly changing temperature</u> inside a nuclear explosion.

3) <u>Intervals</u> between measurements can be more <u>accurate</u> than when a human's doing the measuring — for example a temperature reading taken every 27 seconds will be exactly that.

4) Data loggers don't need tea breaks, lunch breaks or sleep. They can even work during <u>Hollyoaks</u>.

DISADVANTAGES

1) The hardware used for data logging can be <u>very expensive</u> and you may have to buy <u>specialist software</u>.

2) People will need <u>training</u> so they can use the data-logging equipment correctly. This will take <u>time</u> and it could cost <u>money</u>.

3) If the logging equipment <u>malfunctions</u>, you'll <u>lose</u> data — you'll need to <u>back up</u> your data from time to time.

Three trunks, four branches...oh no, that's logging data...

The key things to learn about data logging are the different types of <u>sensor</u>, what information can be collected, the <u>logging period</u> and the <u>logging interval</u>. Just learn that lot and you've got it cracked.

Control Systems

Well lookee what we have here. A fascinating page on basic control systems. Lovely jubbly.

Control Systems are Dedicated or Computer-Controlled

A control system is a system of hardware and software that's used to control the operation of a piece of equipment. There are two main types of control system.

1) Dedicated control systems are basic systems that carry out a pre-programmed set of instructions, e.g. a traffic-light system where the lights change at fixed time intervals.

2) Computer-controlled systems use a computer to control the output device, and this computer can be connected to a sensor — making the system more flexible. These are used in traffic-light systems where the time between changes needs to alter depending on the volume of traffic.

Most Computer Control Systems use Feedback Loops

1) A feedback loop is when information from a sensor is used to control the output of a device. The sensor is often in a different place from the output device. For example, in central heating systems, input from a thermostat (the sensor) is used to control the output of the radiators.

2) Sometimes the feedback data comes from a sensor attached to the output device itself. For example, a robot used to check for leaks inside a sewerage system will send data about its position inside the sewer to a computer, which then uses it to guide the robot's forward movement.

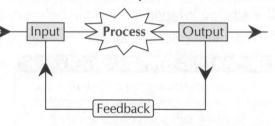

Computer Control Systems need Hardware and Software

1) Sensors are connected to the computer via an interface such as an analogue-to-digital converter (an ADC), or a control board (also called an interface board). This allows the two devices to communicate with each other.

2) The computer then processes the data according to a set of instructions.

3) The output signal from the computer is then sent to the output device. The output will be a digital signal but the output device might only operate using analogue signals — so an output interface containing a digital-to-analogue converter (DAC) might be needed.

4) The output device used will depend on the specific task — but could include a switch or a motor.

EXAMPLE   Making a lamp brighter or dimmer depending on how much natural light there is.

1) A light-dependent resistor is used as the sensor.

2) As less and less light falls on it, its resistance increases.

3) The changing resistance affects the current running through it, which is an analogue signal.

4) An ADC converts this analogue signal into a digital signal, which is processed by a computer.

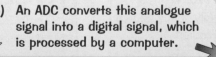

5) The computer's digital output passes through a DAC.

6) The DAC converts the digital output to an analogue voltage.

7) This analogue voltage determines the brightness of the lights.

Where's your sensor humour...

Look on the bright side — once you've passed your exam, you can forget all this stuff. But don't get complacent, you've not passed it yet. Learn it now. Do yourself a favour. Go on.

Control Systems — Two Examples

These examples of control systems should prepare you for the questions you might get in the <u>exam</u>.

Greenhouses Control Environmental Conditions

1) In this diagram of a control system, a <u>heater</u> is controlled by the computer in response to readings from a <u>temperature sensor</u>.

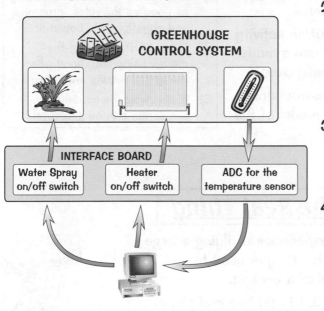

2) When the temperature <u>falls</u> below a certain level, the computer sends a <u>signal</u> to the <u>interface board</u> to <u>switch on</u> the heater. When the desired temperature is reached, the heater's <u>switched off</u> — this is an example of a <u>feedback loop</u>. (<u>Central heating</u> works in the same way.)

3) The <u>water spray</u> is controlled by a simple <u>timer</u> — once the timings have been programmed into the computer, the water spray will be switched on and off at <u>regular intervals</u>.

4) The water spray could be controlled using a <u>feedback loop</u> from a <u>humidity sensor</u> in the soil — but this would make the system more expensive. Other things that could be controlled include opening and closing <u>windows</u>, and the <u>feeding</u> of nutrients to the plants.

5) Fully automated systems are very <u>expensive</u>, so only large greenhouses will have them.

Burglar Alarms Alert People to Intruders

1) Burglar alarms are another good example of a computer control system that uses <u>feedback</u>. Basically the system <u>constantly collects data</u> from <u>input sensors</u>, and when the data suggests that an intruder is present the system sends a signal to an <u>output device</u>.

2) The input sensor might be an <u>infra-red beam</u>, a <u>noise sensor</u>, <u>pressure sensors</u> on the floor or whatever. When the data from one or more sensors exceeds a <u>pre-programmed limit</u>, a signal is sent to an output device, such as a <u>loudspeaker</u> or <u>siren</u>.

3) <u>Automatic doors</u> work in a very similar way. Only the output device is different — it's a <u>motor</u> which opens a door.

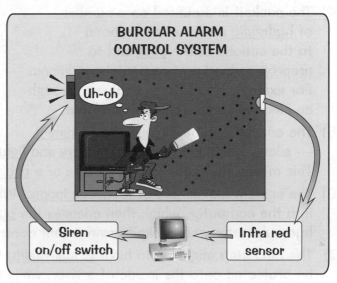

In the ICT Hokey cokey, the right leg is both input and output...

There are loads of other examples of control systems, and all share the same idea — there's an <u>input</u>, which is <u>processed</u> and then there's an <u>output</u>. Think of a video game — the input comes from the controller, it's processed by the console, then there's an output, e.g. a character moving.

Simulations

Flight simulators aim to recreate as closely as possible the experience of flying a <u>real aircraft</u>.

A Simulation is carried out Using a Model

1) A <u>model</u> is an artificial re-creation of an object or phenomenon, and should behave in the <u>same way</u> as the <u>real thing</u> — e.g. a model of a sports car built for testing in a wind tunnel.

2) A <u>simulation</u> is when the model is used to carry out an activity that mimics real life — like when bridge designers use a model to simulate what'll happen when the bridge is actually used.

3) A <u>computer model</u> is created using programmed instructions and equations. An example would be a computer model of the way an aircraft behaves when in flight.

Limitations of Modelling
1) Any model or simulation is only as good as the <u>rules</u>, <u>programs</u> and <u>equations</u> it's based on.
2) It's important to <u>test</u> the model, using situations where the <u>actual</u> results are known.
3) In this way the model and simulation can be <u>improved</u>.

Flight Simulators are Just Like the Real Thing

1) Flight simulators were <u>developed</u> to simulate the experience of flying a large <u>jet aircraft</u> — without the <u>risk</u> of a real plane crash. They're used to <u>train pilots</u>, and are built around a full-scale model of a cockpit.

2) Flight simulators are much <u>safer</u> than teaching a pilot to fly in a real plane. After a 'crash landing', the pilot can simply begin again.

3) Instead of windows there are high resolution <u>computer screens</u> that display computer-generated images. The images work in <u>real time</u> — meaning they respond <u>exactly</u> to the cockpit controls.

4) The cockpit is mounted on a number of <u>hydraulic</u> arms, which respond to the actions of the <u>pilot</u> and to preprogrammed environmental conditions. For example, the effects of flying through an electrical storm can be simulated.

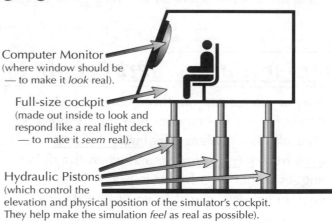

Computer Monitor (where window should be — to make it *look* real).

Full-size cockpit (made out inside to look and respond like a real flight deck — to make it *seem* real).

Hydraulic Pistons (which control the elevation and physical position of the simulator's cockpit. They help make the simulation *feel* as real as possible).

5) The cockpit can be a <u>closed environment</u> — allowing things like <u>cabin pressure</u> and <u>light levels</u> to be as they would in reality. This means that some of the effects of a <u>cabin fire</u> can be simulated.

6) The system makes use of <u>feedback loops</u>. When the pilot alters the controls, signals are input into the computer, which then changes the <u>output</u> of the simulation, e.g. the image screens, hydraulic arms and cockpit environment controls.

7) The next step might be to have <u>virtual-reality</u> flight simulators. The image of the cockpit would be projected onto the inside of a visor, while the pilot's chair would shake about, simulating the movement of the cockpit.

Moving a flight simulator — a load of hydraulics...

There are four main features to a flight simulator — <u>real-time images</u>, <u>hydraulic arms</u>, a <u>closed environment</u> and <u>feedback loops</u> — so learn these, and the effect they have on the final experience.

Robots and Control Language

Don't get your hopes up — we're <u>not</u> talking about robots from space that battle each other. Sorry.

Robots are Usually Computer-Controlled

1) A robot is an <u>automated</u> piece of equipment designed to carry out routine <u>repetitive</u> tasks.

2) Simple robots are designed to carry out a <u>pre-programmed</u> set of operations — like spraying paint onto the bonnet of a car on an assembly line. There are two different ways to <u>develop</u> these instructions.

3) Robots can be programmed to carry out a number of <u>different</u> tasks. For example, a robot could be programmed with different instructions so it can spray different-shaped car bonnets.

4) They usually have some sort of <u>feedback system</u> too, otherwise they're a potential <u>safety hazard</u> — if a robot can't detect that someone's walked in front of the bonnet, the person ends up getting sprayed, not the bonnet.

① The Teach-And-Learn Method
a) The programmer writes a set of instructions.
b) The robot is observed as it carries these instructions out.
c) The instructions are improved if necessary.

② The Do-It-Once-And-Remember-It Method
a) Some robots just need to be guided through the correct movements.
b) They then automatically produce the correct programming instructions to carry out the task.

 Robots
a) are cheaper to operate than paying people wages,
b) don't get tired or make mistakes,
c) carry out tasks that humans can't or won't perform.

Robots
a) can't think for themselves, and so can't respond to new situations as well as humans can,
b) are very expensive to buy.

The Simplest Control Language is LOGO

1) Devices are controlled using special programming <u>languages</u>.

2) A simple example of this kind of language is <u>LOGO</u>, which is sometimes used in schools to introduce the idea of control programs. You can use LOGO to move a <u>turtle</u> on a computer screen — and the trace of the turtle's movements is used to draw an object such as a shape or a letter.

3) You might get asked in the Exam to list some of the simple <u>commands</u> used in LOGO, or to write a simple <u>program</u>. So have a gander at this lot...

> **PROGRAMS AND LANGUAGES**
>
> A <u>program</u> is a sequence of instructions that a computer can carry out.
>
> A <u>programming language</u> is basically the list of commands that the computer will accept.
>
> Programs are eventually translated into <u>machine code</u> — the sequence of 0s and 1s that the computer understands. This is usually done <u>automatically</u>.

Some LOGO commands:
FORWARD X Move turtle forward X units
BACK X Move turtle backward X units
LEFT X Rotate turtle X degrees to the left
RIGHT X Rotate turtle X degrees to the right
REPEAT n [Y] Repeat instruction Y, n times
PENUP Stop drawing a trace
PENDOWN Start drawing a trace

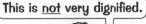

This is <u>not</u> very dignified.

A simple sample LOGO Program:
PENDOWN
FORWARD 40
REPEAT 3 [RIGHT 90 FORWARD 20]
LEFT 45
FORWARD 14
PENUP

Don't Teach-And-Learn, just learn...

Exciting stuff eh? Just like with the rest of this whole book, you've got to get into <u>robot mode</u> and L-E-A-R-N. But not all syllabuses need you to know LOGO commands, so check before you start...

Revision Summary for Section Six

You're looking pretty good — that's another section under your belt. Let's see if everything is under control by simulating a test. Get all these questions right and you'll be a model student. If you make any errors — yep, you've guessed it — go over the stuff you got wrong and then try the questions again.

1) Give a definition of data logging.

2) Explain how a thermistor works.

3) What does CSV stand for? Why is it useful?

4) Explain the difference between a logging period and a logging interval.

5) Give three advantages of using data logging.

6) Give two disadvantages of using data logging.

7) Explain the difference between a dedicated control system and a computer-controlled one.

8) What is a feedback loop? Explain how a feedback loop might work in a smoke alarm.

9) What do the initials ADC and DAC stand for and why are these things needed?

10) Name three sensors you might find in a greenhouse and explain what they might be used for.

11) Describe how a burglar alarm works, using an input and output of your choice.

12) Some buildings have automatic sprinkler systems that spray water in the event of a fire. Explain how sensors and output devices could be used in such a system.

13) Explain the difference between a model and a simulation.

14) What is the main limitation of modelling?

15) Explain fully how a flight simulator works.

16) Describe the teach-and-learn method of programming a robot.

17) Describe the do-it-once-and-remember-it method of programming a robot.

18) Give three reasons why robots might be preferred to human workers.

19) Give two problems with robots.

20) Explain the difference between a programming language and machine code.

21) List four commands used in **LOGO** and explain what they mean.

LAN and WAN

A network is <u>two or more</u> computers <u>connected together</u>. Computers in a network can <u>communicate</u> with each other. The <u>Internet</u> is also a type of network — that's covered in this section too.

LANs are Small, Local Networks

<u>LANs</u> (<u>Local Area Networks</u>) are the networks that you see in most offices and schools.
They have the following hardware:

1) A <u>Network File Server</u> is a computer that runs the software needed by the network, and stores the files that users have created.

2) Individual <u>workstations</u> give users access to the network. They can make use of the network's software and files. Some may need a <u>network interface card</u> to connect to the network, but most now have network hardware built-in.

3) If a group of workstations share a printer then the system needs a <u>print server</u>. If two or more documents are sent to the printer at the same time, the print server will put them into a <u>queue</u>. Users can then <u>carry on with other work</u> whilst waiting for the documents to be printed.

4) For the network to operate, data needs to be sent to and from all parts of the network. This can be done using <u>wire cables</u>, <u>fibre optic cables</u>, or via <u>radio signals</u>.

<u>Note</u> — a LAN doesn't have to include a server. <u>LANs</u> can be as simple as
two or three computers linked together for sharing of files or software.

WANs are Long Range Networks

1) <u>WAN</u> is short for <u>Wide Area Network</u>. They are used when the computers that need to be connected together are in <u>different places</u>.

2) WANs need <u>servers</u> to operate the network. Users connect up to the network from a distance, often using telephone lines. Wireless systems such as <u>microwave links</u> or <u>satellite links</u> can also be used.

3) WANs are used by companies who have <u>employees</u> working <u>away from the firm's main sites</u>. A good example would be oil exploration engineers who work in remote parts of the world. They're also used by firms who have a lot of <u>teleworkers</u> (see p81).

ADVANTAGES of using networks:
1) <u>Peripherals</u> such as <u>printers</u> can be <u>shared</u> amongst many different users.
2) <u>Software</u> can be <u>shared</u> amongst different users.
3) Storing files centrally makes them less vulnerable to loss as a result of workstation <u>failure</u>.
4) <u>Communication</u> across the network is <u>cheap and fast</u>.

DISADVANTAGES of using networks:
1) <u>Cabling</u> can be <u>expensive</u> to <u>install</u> and <u>replace</u>.
2) A <u>fault with a server</u> can <u>prevent</u> the whole network from working.
3) <u>Security</u> measures are needed to <u>restrict access</u> to the network.
4) <u>Viruses</u> could disable the entire network.

Networks — I don' WAN' do this...

All this server talk might be confusing you — a server is just a <u>computer</u> that provides a <u>service</u> to other computers. There are <u>many types</u> of servers, each with a specific function. They might be referred to by their <u>proper name</u>, e.g. 'web server', or just '<u>server</u>'. Make sure you know that.

Network Topologies

Network topologies — ah... I can see you're pretty darn excited. Some of this stuff is a wee bit tricky. But if you give it a bit of thought, the pros and cons of each type are pretty obvious.

Star Networks Give Access to a Central Computer

1) <u>Star networks</u> are used when a <u>large number of workstations</u> need to be connected to a central computer such as a <u>mainframe</u> or <u>server</u>.

2) Each workstation is <u>connected directly</u> to the central computer.

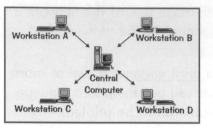

 PROS

1) Performance in one part of the network is unaffected by events <u>elsewhere</u>.

2) It's easy to <u>add more</u> computers to the network.

CONS

1) Failure in the <u>central</u> computer causes the whole network to break down.

2) Uses a lot of cabling, so it's <u>expensive</u>.

Line Networks are the Cheapest

1) In <u>line networks</u> (bus networks) data is sent <u>to and from</u> the file server along a <u>line of cable</u>.

2) All <u>terminals are connected</u> to this central line.

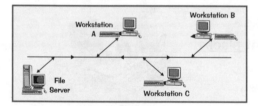

PROS

1) <u>Cheap</u> — because it uses less cabling.

CONS

1) With lots of users the system becomes very <u>slow</u>, as all data goes along a central line.

2) Failure of the central cable will bring the <u>whole</u> network down.

Ring Networks are Faster than Line Networks

1) <u>Ring networks</u> are a <u>bit like line networks</u>, except that all the equipment is <u>linked in a ring</u>.

2) <u>Data flows</u> around the network in <u>one direction only</u>.

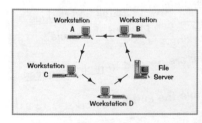

 PROS

1) <u>Cheap</u> to expand.

2) Fast — as data flows in <u>one</u> direction only.

CONS

1) With lots of users the system becomes <u>slower</u>, as all the data is sent along a single line.

2) Failure of the ring cable brings the <u>whole</u> network down.

The definition of lazy — when your net-work is zero...

There's some tricky stuff on this page. But all you need to know are the three most common <u>network topologies</u>, and their <u>pros</u> and <u>cons</u>. Try writing a song or poem about them...it might help.

The Internet

The Internet — known and loved by everyone (except those who are waiting for a file to download).

The Internet is an International Network of Computers

1) The Internet is basically a very big Wide Area Network (WAN) (see page 51 for more).
2) The Internet was originally developed by the US Government to improve communication between its military computers. But it's since grown into what we all know today.

The World Wide Web is only Part of the Internet

1) A lot of people think that the World Wide Web and the Internet are the same thing. Not so.
2) The Web is a system of interlinked documents (web pages) accessed through the Internet.
3) Some of the other major uses of the Internet include e-mail, instant messaging and file sharing.

Getting Connected to the Internet

1) In the early days of home Internet everyone used dial-up connections, which were very slow and meant you couldn't use the phone while connected to the Internet.
2) These days, more and more Internet users have broadband connections, which give much greater download speeds and mean you can still use the phone, yippee...
3) The companies that provide access to the Internet are called ISPs (Internet Service Providers).
4) You need special hardware and software to connect to the Internet and the Web:

Hardware

1) Data from your ISP is sent through a modem (modulator / demodulator) to convert it into a form that can be transmitted, e.g. along telephone lines. A modem connected to your computer converts the data back into a form your computer can understand.
2) If you want a wireless system at home, you can get a wireless modem router (modem and radio transmitter in one). The router connects to the ISP via a phone line, and computers with wireless adaptors connect to the router using radio signals (this is Wi-Fi™).
3) Many mobile devices can access the Internet from anywhere using mobile broadband. Mobile broadband uses mobile phone networks to transfer data to and from the Internet.
4) Most mobile phones can use mobile broadband. You can also buy modems to connect computers to the mobile phone networks that provide mobile broadband.

Software

1) The main piece of software you need to view web pages is a web browser (see page 55).
2) Your browser might need extra software called plug-ins to enable it to view pages with certain types of content, e.g. some animations.

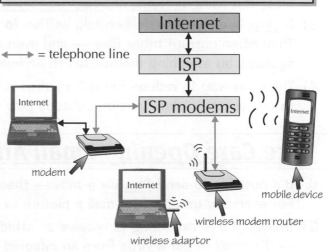

↔ = telephone line

modem

wireless adaptor

wireless modem router

mobile device

5) File servers and print servers (see page 51) can be connected to the Internet.
6) E-mail servers are another type of server — they distribute emails (a bit like a postman).

I wonder what the Outernet is like...

All you need to remember is that the Internet is a massive network and it's not the same as the World Wide Web. Make sure you know about the stuff you need to connect to the Internet, too.

Internet Security

A big problem with the Internet is that data can be <u>intercepted</u> relatively easily by unauthorised users. Exchanging information via phone or digital lines still <u>isn't</u> totally secure. Which is a <u>pain</u>.

On-Line Shopping uses Encryption Software

1) Some people don't like <u>on-line shopping</u> because they're worried that their credit card details might be intercepted and used to make unauthorised purchases. <u>Encryption software</u> can reduce this risk.

> Websites that encrypt details like this are called '<u>secure</u>', and display a <u>padlock</u> icon in the browser.

2) Sensitive information (e.g. credit card details) is <u>encrypted</u> by the website into a code using an <u>algorithm</u> (a set of rules). This code can only be decoded with the right software and a password called a <u>key</u>.

3) In theory, only the retailer's website knows the key, so even if someone intercepts the information, they <u>won't</u> be able to use it.

Passwords give Restricted Access to some Websites

> An <u>intranet</u> is like a private mini-Internet that can only be viewed by people connected to a particular organisation. An <u>extranet</u> is basically an intranet that's connected to the Internet.

1) Some websites restrict access to <u>authorised</u> users only.

2) Schools allowing pupils and parents to access material on their <u>extranet</u> might do this to prevent other people accessing the information.

3) On-line magazines also do this, so they can charge people for access.

4) The usual way to restrict access is to issue <u>user names</u> and <u>passwords</u>.

Get Protection from Hackers and Viruses

1) <u>Hacking</u> means accessing a computer system and its files without permission. It's totally <u>illegal</u>, and once inside a system, the hacker might be able to view, edit, copy or delete important files, or plant a virus.

2) Organisations can protect themselves by using <u>passwords</u>, <u>encrypting</u> files, and using <u>firewalls</u> and <u>hacking-detection</u> software (see page 77).

3) A <u>virus</u> is a program deliberately written to infect a computer, and make <u>copies</u> of itself. They often <u>corrupt</u> other files — and even operating systems. They move between computer systems by attaching themselves to harmless computer files and e-mails (see below).

4) The main way to reduce the risk of viruses is to use <u>anti-virus</u> software — but it's important to use an up-to-date version because new viruses are detected every day.

Take Care Opening Email Attachments

1) It's possible to send <u>files</u> via e-mail — these are called <u>attachments</u>. For example, you could e-mail a picture or a video file to a friend.

2) Unless you're expecting to receive an attachment, treat any you receive with <u>suspicion</u> — it's easy to get a <u>virus</u> from an infected attachment.

3) Some email software lets you <u>view</u> an attachment without downloading it, or use virus-checking software to <u>scan</u> it before opening it. Both help to reduce the risk of getting a virus.

Use encryption software to $MUK)G@S*E your data...

It's a pretty scary world out there. So make sure you know how to <u>protect yourself</u>. Learning the different ways on this page will help you in the <u>exam</u> as well as on the <u>Internet</u>.

Web-Browsing

Even if you think this is all <u>second-nature</u> to you, read it carefully — no slacking...

A Web Browser Displays Web Pages

1) The <u>World Wide Web</u> (see page 53) is made up of <u>a lot</u> of pages — billions and billions.

2) To get your hands on all this information, you need a <u>web browser</u>.

3) It's a piece of <u>software</u> that can <u>understand</u> the code that web pages are made up of, and <u>display</u> the pages in the right way.

A URL is the Address of a Web Page

1) <u>URL</u> stands for <u>Uniform Resource Locator</u> — in other words, the <u>address</u> of a <u>web page</u> (or any other resource on the Internet). For example: http://www.cgpbooks.co.uk

2) You can <u>type</u> a URL <u>directly</u> into a web browser — but some URLs can be extremely <u>long</u> or <u>complicated</u>, so there are <u>other ways</u> to access web pages.

Search Engines and Portals Find Pages

1) <u>Search engines</u> are websites that help you <u>find</u> other websites, <u>without</u> having to know their URL.

2) The <u>basic</u> type of search is a <u>keyword</u> search — you type in a keyword and the search engine <u>lists</u> a load of websites containing that keyword.

3) Or you can do a <u>complex</u> search, using things like <u>AND</u> and <u>OR</u>.

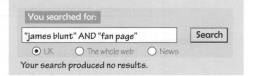

> Most search engines work by storing details or <u>keywords</u> of different websites, but no single search engine will have data on every website — so it's worth using <u>more</u> than one.

4) <u>Portals</u> are websites offering many services in <u>one place</u>, e.g. <u>search engines</u>, <u>e-mail</u> and <u>on-line shopping</u>.

Web Browsers have Features to Help You Browse

BOOKMARKS
Browsers can <u>save</u> URLs you use often as '<u>bookmarks</u>' or '<u>favourites</u>', so you don't have to keep typing them.

STOP AND REFRESH buttons   Stop   Refresh
To <u>prevent</u> your browser from <u>loading</u> the web page it's accessing, you can hit the <u>stop</u> button. To <u>reload</u> a page, use the <u>refresh</u> button.

HOME PAGE
You can set a <u>URL</u> to be accessed as soon as you <u>open</u> a browser — this is the browser's <u>home page</u>. Browsers have a <u>home button</u> that takes you <u>back</u> to the home page.

PHISHING FILTER
<u>Phishing</u> is when people try to get <u>user names</u>, <u>passwords</u>, <u>bank details</u>, etc. by using a web page that <u>looks official</u>. Some browsers look for <u>signs</u> of phishing and <u>prevent</u> you from entering details if a web page is <u>dodgy</u>.

NAVIGATION buttons
You can <u>flick through</u> the pages that you've <u>already looked at</u> by using the <u>back</u> and <u>forward</u> buttons in your browser.

POP-UP BLOCKER
Some browsers automatically <u>block pop-ups</u> — <u>adverts</u> that appear in a <u>new window</u> when you're looking at some web pages.

Web browsing — it's not house-hunting for spiders...

This stuff <u>isn't</u> complicated or difficult, but you need to <u>know</u> all of it. Oh, and it's easy to think that you're an <u>expert</u> because you've used a search engine before, but that <u>might not</u> be the case...

E-Mail

That's right, it's time to learn the <u>basics</u> of something that you probably use on a daily basis. Enjoy...

E-Mail is Electronic Mail

1) E-mail is a way of <u>sending messages</u> (and files) from one computer to another.

2) You need an <u>e-mail account</u> to send and receive e-mails — you can usually get one from your <u>ISP</u> or from a <u>web-based e-mail service</u>.

3) Your account is identified by its <u>e-mail address</u>, e.g. cgpbooks@cgpbooks.co.uk. The bit <u>before</u> the @ sign is <u>personalised</u> — the bit <u>after</u> tells you the e-mail account <u>provider</u>.

No, that's a fe-mail.

4) An e-mail address is like a <u>postal address</u>, so people can direct a message to you by sending it to your e-mail address. Messages are collected in the <u>inbox</u> of your account.

5) After you've read an email, you can <u>reply</u> to it, <u>forward</u> it on to someone else, <u>store</u> it away in a folder (see below) or <u>delete</u> it.

Creating and Sending an E-Mail is Simple

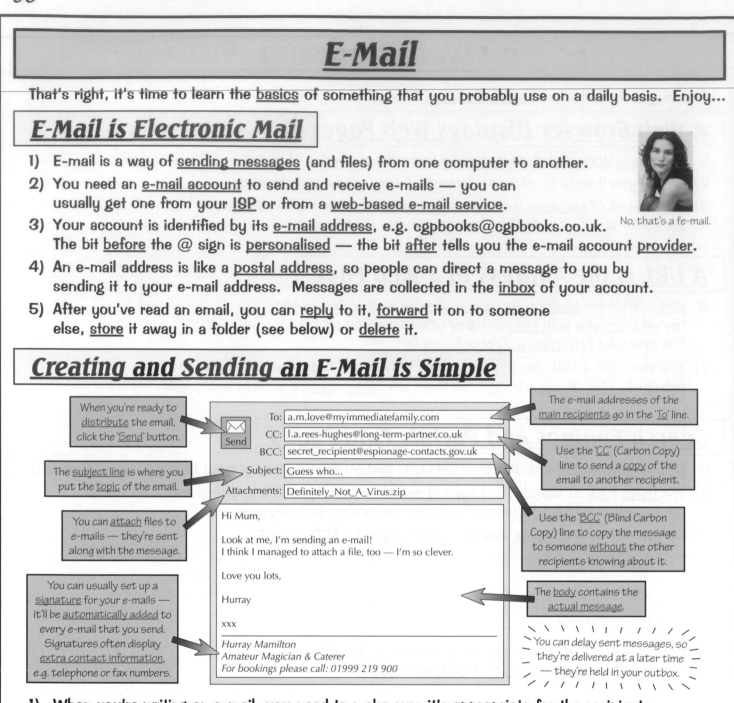

When you're ready to <u>distribute</u> the email, click the '<u>Send</u>' button.

The e-mail addresses of the <u>main recipients</u> go in the '<u>To</u>' line.

The <u>subject line</u> is where you put the <u>topic</u> of the email.

Use the '<u>CC</u>' (Carbon Copy) line to send a <u>copy</u> of the email to another recipient.

You can <u>attach</u> files to e-mails — they're sent along with the message.

Use the '<u>BCC</u>' (Blind Carbon Copy) line to copy the message to someone <u>without</u> the other recipients knowing about it.

You can usually set up a <u>signature</u> for your e-mails — it'll be <u>automatically added</u> to every e-mail that you send. Signatures often display <u>extra contact information</u>, e.g. telephone or fax numbers.

The <u>body</u> contains the <u>actual message</u>.

You can delay sent messages, so they're delivered at a later time — they're held in your outbox.

To: a.m.love@myimmediatefamily.com
CC: l.a.rees-hughes@long-term-partner.co.uk
BCC: secret_recipient@espionage-contacts.gov.uk
Subject: Guess who...
Attachments: Definitely_Not_A_Virus.zip

Hi Mum,

Look at me, I'm sending an e-mail!
I think I managed to attach a file, too — I'm so clever.

Love you lots,

Hurray

xxx

Hurray Mamilton
Amateur Magician & Caterer
For bookings please call: 01999 219 900

1) When you're writing an e-mail, you need to make sure it's <u>appropriate</u> for the recipients.

2) For example, if it's a <u>business</u> e-mail you should use a <u>formal style</u> and <u>formal language</u>.

3) E-mails to <u>friends</u> and <u>family</u> can be <u>light-hearted</u>, e.g. use different font colours and silly pictures.

E-Mail Software can Manage Messages and Contacts

1) Nearly all e-mail software lets you create different <u>folders</u> to store e-mails in.

2) Some software will automatically <u>filter junk</u> e-mails out of your inbox.

3) <u>Junk mail</u> (or <u>spam</u>) is <u>unsolicited</u> (not asked for) and usually <u>advertises</u> things, e.g. pharmaceuticals — but the sellers are as <u>dodgy</u> as a geezer operating out of a suitcase in Peckam.

4) Most e-mail software lets you <u>manage</u> your <u>contacts</u>, so you can <u>store</u> the e-mail addresses of people that you e-mail <u>regularly</u>. You can also create <u>mailing lists</u>, which are <u>groups</u> of e-mail addresses — useful when you're sending out regular messages to <u>lots</u> of people.

Eee, mail just isn't what it used to be — no stamps, for one...

<u>Don't</u> assume that just because you've sent an e-mail that you'll be able to answer <u>any question</u> about the stuff above. <u>Learn it all</u> as if it were a page on quantum mechanics or thermodynamics.

Modern Communication Methods

Face-to-face talking is <u>so</u> last century — you need to know about a few of the more <u>hi-tech ways</u> that you can <u>communicate</u> with other people. I doubt this will be enlightening, but bear with me...

Mobile Phones Can Send Text Messages Using SMS

1) <u>Mobile phones</u> can be used to send <u>SMS text messages</u> (<u>SMS</u> stands for <u>Short Message Service</u>).

2) Single messages can be up to <u>160 characters</u> long, but you can string multiple messages together.

3) They're <u>fiddly</u> to type, and people often <u>abbreviate</u> words using textspeak.
This makes them most useful for <u>short</u>, <u>informal</u> messages.

Instant Messaging is like Texting over the Internet

Typing messages in <u>real time</u> over the <u>Internet</u>
is called <u>instant messaging</u>.

> <u>Chat rooms</u> are a sort of <u>open</u> instant messaging conversation — <u>anyone</u> can enter a chat room and talk to people who are connected to the same room. It's <u>hard</u> to <u>control</u> who talks to who in chat rooms — which raises concerns about <u>children's safety</u>.

1) As long as both users are <u>connected</u> to the Internet, they can receive messages from the other <u>instantaneously</u>.

2) You can make it even more personal by using <u>webcams</u> or by sending and receiving <u>audio</u> in real time like a phone call.

3) Instant messaging services let you <u>add</u> or <u>remove</u> people from a personal <u>contacts list</u> so you're in control of who can contact you.

Forums are like Places for Discussion

Lots of websites have forums, where people usually discuss topics related to the website's content. Forums are made up of individual <u>threads</u> (a question or comment and all its posted responses).

> <u>Bulletin boards</u> are like forums, but they're usually used for <u>announcements</u>, e.g. adverts and details of events.

1) Forums are run by <u>administrators</u> and <u>moderators</u>. They're responsible for keeping messages <u>appropriate</u>, and for monitoring users.

2) Users normally have to <u>register</u> to post (leave) comments — some sites ask for a lot of details, some only a <u>username</u> and <u>password</u>. On most you have to accept some <u>terms and conditions</u> before posting anything.

3) Forums usually display all the previous comments on the topic in <u>order</u>, with any new contributions appearing at the <u>bottom</u> of the thread.

VoIP lets you Call People Using the Internet

1) <u>VoIP</u> stands for <u>Voice over Internet Protocol</u> — it sounds complicated, but it's just a way of having a voice conversation with someone over the Internet.

2) A <u>traditional</u> phone call involves <u>sending</u> and <u>receiving</u> voices through a telephone system — a VoIP call just sends everything via <u>the Internet</u>.

3) VoIP calls are generally <u>cheaper</u> than traditional phone calls, or even 'free' (after you've taken into account how much it costs you to access the Internet).

Instant messaging — why wait for mundane information?

All these technologies are marvellous, but it makes it harder to <u>avoid</u> talking to people you really don't want to. My <u>advice</u> — find a <u>quiet</u> corner, stick your head in this book and <u>get learning</u>...

Social Networking

If you use forums and instant messaging services you can be quite <u>anonymous</u> and not share much personal information — but social networking websites rely on <u>customised</u> webpages.

Networking Websites Combine Interactive Features

Social networks are <u>big business</u> in the Internet world.
Most <u>social network websites</u> contain a <u>mixture</u> of:

1) An <u>email</u> service.

2) <u>Instant messaging</u>.

3) A way to publish original material like <u>blogs</u>.

4) <u>Forums</u> or groups designed for people with a <u>certain interest</u>.

5) Facilities for <u>sharing files</u> (like music or videos) or website <u>links</u> with other members.

6) Ways to chat over <u>webcams</u> or make <u>voice calls</u> over the Internet.

> Blog is short for <u>web log</u> — a blog is just a collection of messages over time on a certain subject, e.g. a person's day or world news. Blogs can be <u>read</u> and <u>commented</u> on by other people.

Some Websites Let You Create an Entire Profile

When you've <u>registered</u> with certain websites, you can <u>create a profile</u>.

1) Users upload a <u>photo</u> or <u>picture</u> of themselves to be their profile photo.

2) You can add <u>personal details</u>, e.g. age, town of birth, schools, etc.

3) You can also add lots of other <u>information</u> about yourself, e.g. hobbies, music tastes, sports, pets, shoe size, favourite herb or spice... anything.

Barney126's profile pic.
Even dogs can have their own profiles. (I kid you not...)

Social networks also have <u>search</u> facilities so you can find other users to <u>link</u> your profile to. You can search a number of different fields — the most common is someone's <u>name</u>, but you can search by <u>email</u> or <u>username</u>, as well as by <u>location</u> or by an <u>interest</u> you might share. A link is only established when <u>both</u> users have <u>confirmed</u> they are happy to do so.

Social Networks have Advantages and Disadvantages

ADVANTAGES (mainly social)	DISADVANTAGES (mainly security or privacy)
1) Social networks are <u>country</u> and <u>world-wide</u>. You can <u>keep up</u> with friends all over the place, and even make <u>new</u> ones.	Most social networking websites let you change <u>privacy settings</u> but:
2) They can be a good place for people to be <u>creative</u> and get pieces of their own work noticed.	1) You can still share too much information and put yourself at <u>risk</u> from things like identity theft.
3) Large networks are brilliant for <u>raising awareness</u> about charity appeals, sponsored events, and other good causes.	2) Friends made through the website might <u>lie</u> about themselves. 3) <u>Employers</u> have been accused of letting the profiles become a factor in their eventual decision about <u>job applications</u>.

Some information you should definitely keep to yourself...

...like the fact that I wear a bright yellow wig when I clean my kitchen. Social networks are mainly for interacting with friends, but it's best to <u>be careful</u> — don't give nasty people any opportunities.

Digital TV Systems

TV has come along way since it was first invented — you need to know what it's like now.

Digital TV is the New Standard of Broadcasting

1) Digital TV has a few advantages over old analogue TV broadcasts — the quality of pictures and sounds is higher, more channels can be broadcast and programmes can be interactive (e.g. different camera angles, commentary, etc.).

2) Another feature of digital TV is an Electronic Programme Guide (EPG) — it's basically an interactive TV guide showing what's on over the next week or two.

3) Digital TV is delivered to people's homes in one of three main ways:

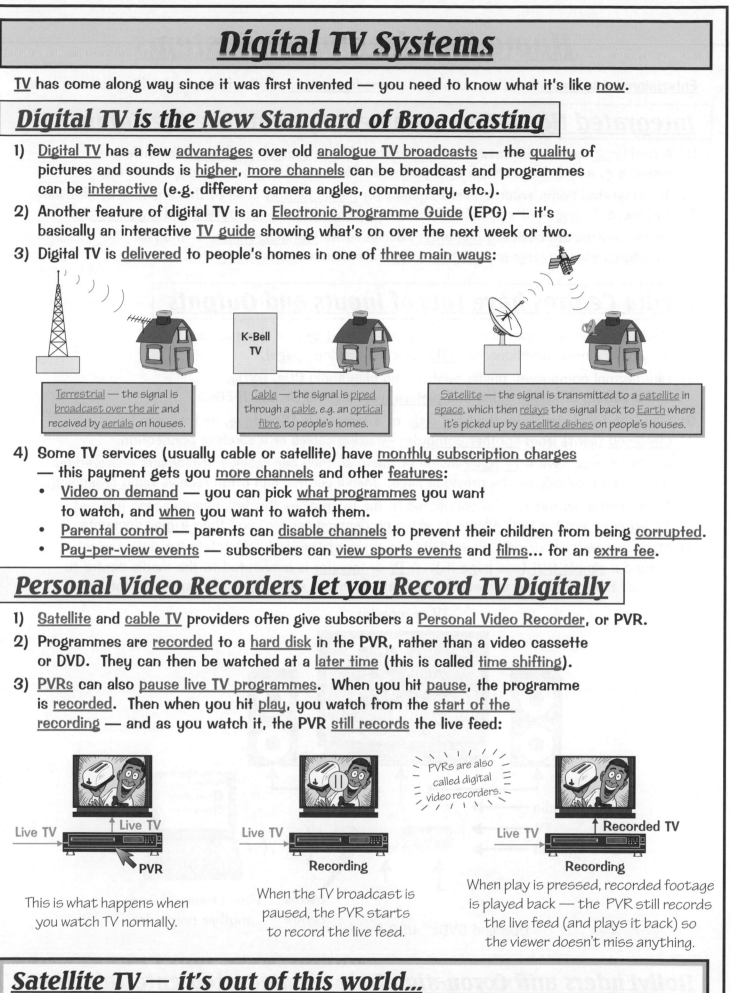

Terrestrial — the signal is broadcast over the air and received by aerials on houses.

Cable — the signal is piped through a cable, e.g. an optical fibre, to people's homes.

Satellite — the signal is transmitted to a satellite in space, which then relays the signal back to Earth where it's picked up by satellite dishes on people's houses.

4) Some TV services (usually cable or satellite) have monthly subscription charges — this payment gets you more channels and other features:
   - Video on demand — you can pick what programmes you want to watch, and when you want to watch them.
   - Parental control — parents can disable channels to prevent their children from being corrupted.
   - Pay-per-view events — subscribers can view sports events and films... for an extra fee.

Personal Video Recorders let you Record TV Digitally

1) Satellite and cable TV providers often give subscribers a Personal Video Recorder, or PVR.

2) Programmes are recorded to a hard disk in the PVR, rather than a video cassette or DVD. They can then be watched at a later time (this is called time shifting).

3) PVRs can also pause live TV programmes. When you hit pause, the programme is recorded. Then when you hit play, you watch from the start of the recording — and as you watch it, the PVR still records the live feed:

PVRs are also called digital video recorders.

Live TV → Live TV — PVR

This is what happens when you watch TV normally.

Live TV — Recording

When the TV broadcast is paused, the PVR starts to record the live feed.

Live TV → Recorded TV — Recording

When play is pressed, recorded footage is played back — the PVR still records the live feed (and plays it back) so the viewer doesn't miss anything.

Satellite TV — it's out of this world...

Boo to all this digital nonsense — bring back the humble VCR, with added entertainment features such as tracking adjustment and rewinding tapes back to the beginning. The fun I used to have...

Home Entertainment Systems

Entertainment systems have also changed — media centres are the fashionable thing to have now...

Integrated Home Entertainment Systems are the Future

1) A traditional home entertainment system would have separate hardware for different tasks, e.g. a hi-fi for music, a DVD player for films, a set-top box for digital TV, etc.

2) An integrated home entertainment system (or media centre) is all of those pieces of hardware, and more, in one — it's possible thanks to advanced home computers and digital media.

3) Media centres are basically computers designed for watching media — they're usually smaller, quieter and simpler to operate than a normal computer.

Media Centres have Lots of Inputs and Outputs

1) Media centres, like normal computers, have a hard disk — this means they have similar functions to PVRs (see the previous page).

2) Like normal computers, media centres can play audio CDs, DVDs, and a variety of audio, video and picture files, e.g. MP3s and JPEGs.

3) Files can be played from the hard disk, or a removable USB drive, or they can be streamed (sent) from another computer — using cables or a wireless connection.

4) Media centres have a TV tuner inside of them, so they can receive broadcasts delivered by one of the methods on the previous page. Media centres can often receive radio broadcasts.

5) Many media centres can be connected to the Internet — this lets users access Internet TV services like the BBC iPlayer (a video on demand service) and their e-mail accounts.

6) Media centres are usually controlled by one remote control, which lets the user navigate around a simple GUI (see page 15). A TV or monitor is connected to the media centre to view all the media, and sometimes separate speakers and an amplifier are used for audio.

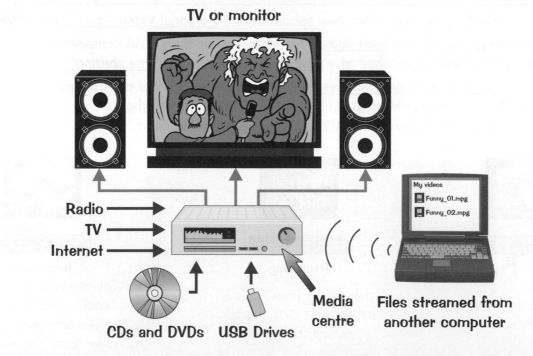

TV or monitor

Radio
TV
Internet

CDs and DVDs   USB Drives

Media centre

Files streamed from another computer

My videos
Funny_01.mpg
Funny_02.mpg

HollyEnders and Coronation Dale — integrated entertainment...

I don't know about you, but I'm feeling kinda sleepy. Luckily it's the last page of stuff you'll have to absorb for this section. That can only mean one thing — it's time for a pop quiz, hotshot...

Revision Summary for Section Seven

Well, you knew it was coming so don't try to act all surprised. Like with all the other sets of questions, try your hardest to answer each question — if you get it right, you will be granted access to the next question (what a treat). If you don't know the answer, retrace your steps back to the page in question and learn it all like you've never learned before. Right then, here we go...

1) What do the letters LAN and WAN stand for?

2) What's the difference between a LAN and a WAN?

3) Explain two advantages and two disadvantages of connecting computers in a network.

4) Sketch a diagram of a star network, a line network and a ring network.

5) Which of these types of network uses the most cable?

6) Which two types of network are the slowest?

7) Explain the difference between the Internet and the World Wide Web.

8) Name the old-fashioned and modern ways of connecting to the Internet.

9) What does ISP stand for?

10) Explain what a modem does.

11) Describe two types of server that are connected to the Internet.

12) Describe how on-line shopping can be made less risky.

13) What is an intranet and how can you restrict access to one?

14) Explain what hacking is and describe one way that a company can protect itself from hacking.

15) How can you reduce the risk of getting a virus from an e-mail attachment?

16) What kind of software is needed to view web pages?

17) What does URL stand for?

18) How can you access web pages without knowing their URL?

19) Describe three features of a web browser that help you to navigate the Web.

20) What do you need before you can start to send and receive emails.

21) Describe one use of an e-mail signature.

22) What do CC and BCC stand for?

23) What is junk mail?

24) What is a mailing list?

25) Describe three modern methods of communication.

26) Name three things that you might find on a social networking website.

27) Describe one advantage and one disadvantage of social networking websites.

28) Give two advantages of digital TV over analogue TV.

29) Explain three common features of satellite and cable TV services.

30) Describe what's going on inside a PVR when you pause and resume live TV programmes.

31) Describe four features of an integrated home entertainment system.

Systems Life Cycle and Systems Analysis

This is perhaps the scariest bit of ICT — changing <u>existing information systems</u> into <u>new and improved ones</u>. A brief overview first... specifics later on. Have fun.

A System Life Cycle Shows How a System Changes

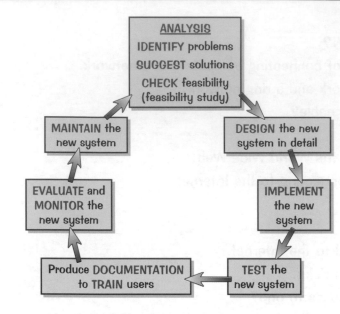

ANALYSIS
IDENTIFY problems
SUGGEST solutions
CHECK feasibility
(feasibility study)

DESIGN the new system in detail

IMPLEMENT the new system

TEST the new system

Produce DOCUMENTATION to TRAIN users

EVALUATE and MONITOR the new system

MAINTAIN the new system

The diagram on the left is a <u>system life cycle</u> — the different <u>stages</u> that you go through when developing a <u>new ICT system</u>.

Familiarise yourself with it — it'll help you to see how all the bits in this section fit together.

It also makes the <u>important point</u> that the job <u>isn't finished</u> when the new system has been <u>implemented</u> — the new system will eventually become less useful, and the whole cycle begins again. What fun.

I'm a cisterns analyst

An information system is just a way of inputting, storing, processing and outputting data.

The term <u>systems analysis</u> is often used to describe the <u>analysis</u> and <u>design</u> stages.

Systems Analysis Involves Identifying Problems

1) There are <u>two main types of problems</u> with existing systems.
Firstly, there might be problems with a <u>manual system</u> where introducing a computerised system would make things better. Secondly, there might be problems because the <u>existing computer</u> system is <u>unable to cope</u> with the information processing demanded of it.

2) In order to identify the problems the systems analyst needs to

I just can't cope with the information processing demanded of me.

- <u>interview</u> users of the system to find out their experiences;
- <u>analyse</u> the results of questionnaires given to the users;
- <u>observe</u> people using the system;
- <u>study</u> documents such as user guides, printouts and error reports.

3) From this research the systems analyst should <u>understand</u> how the present system works and what the <u>problems</u> are.

4) This information is then used to <u>work out</u> how a <u>new system</u> could be put together that would <u>solve</u> these problems.
There's more about this side of systems analysis on the <u>next page</u>.

Identify the problem — GCSEs, they're the problem...

Learn that <u>circle diagram</u> thingy. It's a really good <u>summary</u> of what this whole section's about, which is useful because it's easy to get lost in the world of <u>ICT systems</u>. I'm still trapped in there...

More Systems Analysis

OK, so you've found out that your <u>existing system</u> isn't that brilliant any more. In that case you'll need to come up with a <u>new system</u> to solve the problems.

Systems Analysis Also Involves Suggesting Solutions

1) The <u>other side</u> of <u>systems analysis</u> means coming up with a <u>new system</u> that <u>solves</u> the problems in the existing system.

2) The systems analyst will set <u>several objectives</u> for the new system, and then come up with a design to <u>achieve</u> those objectives.

3) At this stage in the life cycle, the systems analyst has a <u>rough idea</u> of how to make the new system, but <u>nothing concrete</u>. All the details will follow later, once a <u>feasibility study</u> has been carried out.

> • <u>Objectives</u> are <u>specific outcomes</u> that can be used to <u>test</u> whether the new system is an <u>improvement</u> on the existing one. They're also called <u>performance criteria</u> and <u>evaluation criteria</u>.
>
> • An <u>example objective</u> would be, "reduce the time needed to process the data by 25%". This is a good objective because it can be tested by <u>measuring</u> and then <u>comparing</u> the time taken on the old and new systems.

A Feasibility Study Checks the New System is Worthwhile

1) When you've got the basics of the new system down, you need to work out <u>if</u> making it will be (i) <u>possible</u> and (ii) <u>worthwhile</u>...

2) This is where a <u>feasibility study</u> comes in (the last part of the <u>analysis stage</u>):

> **(i) Is it <u>possible</u> to make the new system?**
> A systems analyst has to look at and <u>compare</u> all of the <u>hardware</u>, <u>software</u> and <u>trained people</u> available to them, and then decide if the new system can actually be made.

> **(ii) Will the <u>benefits</u> of making and operating the new system be <u>greater</u> than the <u>costs</u>?**
> This is known as a <u>cost-benefit analysis</u> — it takes into account things like the cost of <u>new equipment</u> and the increase in overall <u>efficiency</u>, as well as the less obvious things, e.g. the cost of <u>redundancies</u> and <u>retraining</u>.

3) A feasibility study is usually based on '<u>best guesses</u>' — it's very hard to be <u>certain</u> about <u>everything</u> without actually building the new system. But without some guesses at this stage you <u>won't</u> be able to <u>estimate</u> the likely <u>cost</u> of the new system.

The Feasibility Study is Presented to the Decision-Makers

1) The <u>feasibility study</u> needs to be <u>presented</u> to the people who will have to <u>decide</u> whether or not to <u>proceed</u> with the new system. These are often <u>company directors</u> or <u>senior managers</u>.

2) <u>Sometimes</u> a number of <u>different solutions</u> will be recommended.

And so I recommend that you sell off all your playing fields and give all your pupils a free laptop.

Do we need a colder ice box — let's do a freezeability study...

So, that's the <u>analysis stage</u> polished off. Make sure you know about both <u>systems analysis</u> and <u>feasibility studies</u> — they're both important, as their <u>outcomes</u> decide if a new system <u>goes ahead</u>.

Design — Input, Process and Output

Once you've been given the go ahead by the head honchos, it's time to start fleshing out the new system. The next few pages are all about the design stage of the system life cycle.

Input — How the Data is Captured

1) This involves thinking about methods of data capture (p72).

2) It also means thinking about the format of that data. For example, the input data might need to be organised into fields of fixed or variable length.

3) The use of codes can reduce the file size. For example, a person's gender can be entered as M or F — reducing the number of bytes needed to store the data.

4) Forms should be sketched showing what the user will see whilst they input the data.

Input Checklist

Decide where the data will come from. ☐

Design the data capture forms. ☐

Decide how the data needs to be structured. ☐

Decide how the data will be input. ☐

Design the input screen. ☐

Decide how the data will be validated. ☐

Process — What Happens to It

Process Checklist

List the tasks that need to be done. ☐

Write the processes that enable them to be done. ☐

Produce a plan to test if the processing works. ☐

1) The tasks that the system needs to perform should be based on the original problem and objectives.

2) The processes needed to carry out each task might include spreadsheet formulas, database searches, desktop publishing page design, and word-processing mail-merge routines.

3) The processes could also include exchanging data between different applications. For example, importing a spreadsheet and using it to create a table in a word-processing package.

4) Test plans check that things work as expected. A test plan for the field 'month of birth' might include using normal data such as 6, extreme data such as 12 and invalid data such as Boris (see p67). This will test whether the data validation works.

Output — Let it Out

1) The Golden Rule is to be user-friendly. This means that the output must be appropriate for the needs of the audience.

2) Users should only be shown the information that they need — and it should be communicated in a way they will easily understand. Layout is as important as content.

I say old chap, could you ascertain whether my internal-combustion-engine-driven automobile possesses an erroneous vulcanised-rubber revolving device?

3) The layout of output screens and printouts should first be sketched in rough. They should then be shown to the user to check they are OK.

Output Checklist

Decide which data needs to be output. ☐

Decide how to present the information. ☐

Decide which output devices to use. ☐

Design output screens. ☐

Input, output, shake-it-all-about-put...

There might only be three stages, but don't let that fool you — there's a lot of stuff to consider when you're talking about inputs, processes and outputs. Only move on when you know the lot.

Design — Top-Down and Data-Flow

It's dead important to know how all the bits of the system fit together. The three types of diagram on the next two pages show how this can be done. Make sure you know the differences between them.

Top-Down Diagrams Set Out the Main Tasks

1) Top-down design looks at the whole system by identifying the main tasks to be done and then breaking them down into smaller tasks.

2) If you read a top-down design from top to bottom each big task is broken down into smaller tasks. Reading it from left to right tells you the order in which they happen.

3) Top-down diagrams show what has to happen — but they don't always show how they'll happen.

4) The example below shows the tasks needed to create and print a copy of a new database record.

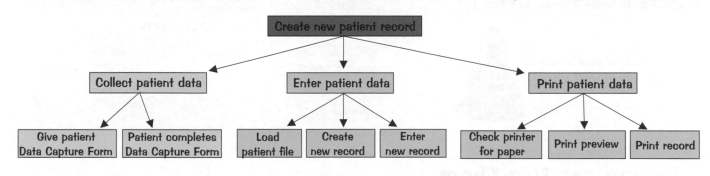

Data-Flow Diagrams Show What Happens to the Data

1) Data-flow diagrams show how data moves around the system — and what happens to it at each stage. There are three main symbols used.

2) The rectangle shows where data has come from. The sausage shows a process such as a search. The square shows where the data is stored — this can include a manual store of a hard copy.

3) Data-flow diagrams show what happens to the data — but they don't show what hardware and software are needed to make this happen.

4) The example shows how an optician can send reminder letters to people who have not had an eye test within the past year.

5) This is a data-flow diagram for just one task. A whole system could be shown by linking together the separate diagrams for each task — rather like linking up different people's family trees.

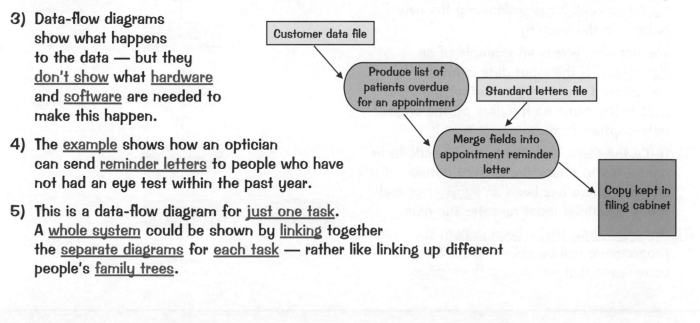

Top-down — the best feathers to fill your duvet...

It's unlikely you'll be asked to draw one of these in the exam. However you might get shown one and asked questions about it. So make sure you can turn these diagrams into written instructions.

Design — System Flowcharts

Most people find these incredibly <u>scary</u>. But they're pretty straightforward really.
Once you know what the symbols mean all you've got to do is practise <u>drawing</u> them.

Learn the Symbols...

System flowcharts show exactly how the data will move through the system.

The <u>symbol</u> for <u>stored data</u> is sometimes <u>replaced</u> by one of the <u>other magenta symbols</u> if the analyst wants to <u>specify</u> the type of <u>storage medium</u> to be used. (The colours used here aren't standard — they're just to make it easier to follow.)

> I see a tall dark wardrobe, and lots of shelf space...

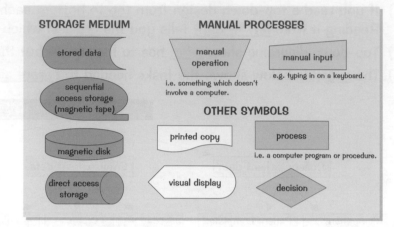

STORAGE MEDIUM

- stored data
- sequential access storage (magnetic tape)
- magnetic disk
- direct access storage

MANUAL PROCESSES

- manual operation — i.e. something which doesn't involve a computer.
- manual input — e.g. typing in on a keyboard.

OTHER SYMBOLS

- printed copy
- process — i.e. a computer program or procedure.
- visual display
- decision

...so you can Use Them

1) Here's an <u>example</u> of a system flowchart for creating a <u>new patient record</u> at a dentist's surgery.

2) The customer completes a <u>data-capture form</u>. This information is then <u>entered</u> onto the patient record file <u>by the receptionist</u>.

3) The new patient record is then <u>used to create a mail-merged letter</u> welcoming the new patient to the surgery.

4) The decision box is an example of an <u>algorithm</u>. If the input data is invalid the receptionist must <u>verify</u> whether the input data is the same as the data on the original data-capture form.

5) If it's the same then the patient needs to be contacted to check the correct details. If it's different there has been an <u>input error</u> and the receptionist must re-enter the data.

6) <u>Once the flowchart's been drawn</u>, the programmer will be able to write the commands that will <u>create the system</u>.

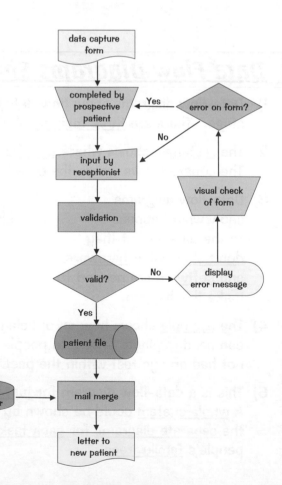

Computer scientists dance to the beat of algorithms...

You really need to practise drawing these charts. <u>Step one</u> — memorise and copy out all the symbols. <u>Step two</u> — memorise and copy out the flowchart on this page. <u>Step three</u> — draw a system flowchart for the diagrams on the previous page. <u>Step four</u> — go and have a lie down.

Implementation and Testing

When you've got your new system ready to go, it's time to <u>implement</u> it. But you'll need to keep <u>testing</u> it, to make sure that you uncover any <u>problems</u> that might stop the software from working.

There are Three Different Ways to Implement the System

<u>Implementation</u> happens when <u>data</u> from the old system is <u>loaded onto the new system</u>, and the new system is <u>used</u> to carry out the task it was <u>designed</u> for. There are <u>three different ways</u> of timing the introduction of the new system — each with its <u>benefits and problems</u>.

1) <u>Direct implementation</u> is when the old system is <u>decommissioned</u> and the new system <u>started up</u> at the <u>same time</u>. There is <u>no change-over period</u> so the users need to be able to use the new system straight away.

An <u>advantage</u> is that the <u>benefits</u> of the new system happen <u>as quickly as possible</u>.

A <u>disadvantage</u> is that any <u>bugs</u> not picked up during testing could have <u>disastrous effects</u>.

2) <u>Phased implementation</u> is when <u>different parts</u> of the system are <u>introduced one at a time</u>. The <u>old system</u> is <u>kept running</u> while this happens.

A <u>plus</u> point is that any problems with the <u>new system</u> can be identified and fixed one at a time, causing <u>less disruption</u> overall.

A <u>snag</u> is that it can take a long time <u>to introduce</u> the new system this way — so the <u>benefits</u> take a <u>long time</u> to come through.

3) <u>Parallel implementation</u> is when the <u>new system</u> is introduced <u>all in one go</u> — but the <u>old system</u> is <u>kept running</u> whilst the new one is tested. This means that for a while there are <u>two systems</u>.

A <u>benefit</u> is that the new system can be <u>tested very quickly</u> — and <u>problems</u> can be sorted out <u>without</u> important operations being affected.

2 tons
A <u>problem</u> is that all <u>tasks</u> need to be <u>done twice</u>.

There are Two Types of Test to be Done...

1) <u>System testing</u> checks whether or not the system will work. One way is to use <u>test data</u>.
   - <u>Invalid data</u> (erroneous data) is anything that the <u>system should reject</u>.
   - <u>Normal data</u> is anything that <u>should work</u> in the system.
   - <u>Extreme data</u> is data that should work but is at the edge of what is acceptable, e.g. entering the <u>largest</u> numbers that a field can accept.

Normal office attire Extreme office attire Invalid office attire

2) Any part of the system that doesn't work is said to have a <u>bug</u> — testing enables the programmer to know which parts of the system need to be <u>debugged</u>.

3) <u>Acceptance testing</u> checks whether the system <u>meets the needs</u> of the users. This <u>might involve a trial run</u> with real users — which can help the programmers make the system more user-friendly.

ICT systems are starting to test my patience...

There's been some tough old stuff in this section — but this wasn't a bad page. Why not write a mini-essay about <u>implementing</u> and <u>testing</u> a new piece of software. Go on...you know you want to.

Documentation, Evaluation and Maintenance

People need <u>training</u> to use a new system <u>effectively</u>. This is where the <u>user documentation</u> steps in.

User Documentation Explains How to Operate the System

As the name suggests, user documents are written to help the people who will use the system. There are <u>three types of guide</u> — depending on when they might be needed.

1) <u>Installation guides</u> explain how the system should be <u>installed</u> and programs <u>loaded</u> — as well as which <u>peripherals</u> are needed and how they should be <u>installed</u>.

2) <u>User guides</u> give instructions on how to <u>perform tasks</u> using the system — for example how to carry out searches and print data from a database.

3) <u>Tutorials</u> are short <u>training manuals</u> explaining how the system works. They might include <u>exercises</u> which help the user to <u>practise</u> operating the software.

User documentation can be <u>hard to write</u>. This is because it needs to be written in <u>simple language</u> so the users can understand what they have to do — but at the same time it needs to use the same <u>technical terms</u> that are used in the software.

Evaluation Checks if the System Still Meets its Objectives

1) Once the system is installed its performance will be <u>monitored</u> to see whether it's working properly. From time to time it'll be <u>evaluated</u>. This is a check to <u>see if the system still meets its objectives</u> — in other words whether it still does what it was designed to do.

2) <u>Evaluation</u> is basically <u>repeating</u> the <u>research carried out at the start</u> of the system life cycle. In other words <u>observing</u> and <u>interviewing</u> users and <u>studying</u> printouts.

3) One reason why the system might <u>not</u> meet its objectives is if the <u>workload increases</u>. The <u>demands</u> on the system may become <u>greater than</u> its <u>ability</u> to cope. In other words it becomes <u>obsolete</u>. This brings the system life cycle <u>full circle</u> and the analyst is brought back to begin work on a <u>new system</u>.

Technical Documentation Explains How to Maintain it

Technical documentation is written for the <u>computer engineers and programmers</u> who will maintain the system after it's been installed. Since they're computer experts, the guides can be <u>full of technical language and complex system diagrams</u>. There are two times when it's needed.

1) When something goes wrong and the system needs to be repaired. The technical manual should <u>enable fault finding</u> to take place — in other words, tell the engineer what's wrong. It should then <u>explain how to fix it</u>.

2) When the system needs <u>upgrading</u> — for example, installing a better user interface. The computer engineer needs to know <u>how this can be done</u>.

It says here, try adjusting the brightness...

My evaluation — making ICT systems ~~really sucks~~ is great...

I think I'm spoiling you with this kind of page — nothing difficult, just a few <u>specific terms</u> and <u>common sense</u>. So that's this section done...oh wait, there's a <u>gift</u> for you just over the page...

Revision Summary for Section Eight

Well done, you made it to the end of Section Eight. Now you know all about making new systems — or do you? This stuff's really important in the world of ICT, so it's pretty likely that you'll get asked some questions about it in your exam. So, roll up your sleeves, grasp the nettle and take the bull by the horns — there are some tough questions coming up.

1) What is your name? Sorry, only kidding. What comes between analysing and implementing a new computer system?

2) List three ways of gathering information about the problems of an old system.

3) As well as finding problems with old systems, what else does a systems analyst do?

4) What is the difference between objectives, performance criteria and evaluation criteria?

5) What is a feasibility study for?

6) What question does a cost-benefit analysis try to answer?

7) List three things that should be done when designing a system's input.

8) List three things that should be done when designing a system's processes.

9) List three things that should be done when designing a system's output.

10) In which two ways do you read a top-down diagram?

11) What does it mean if you see a sausage on a data-flow diagram?
    a) Input   b) Process   c) You've dropped your dinner again.

12) Correctly label each symbol in the box.

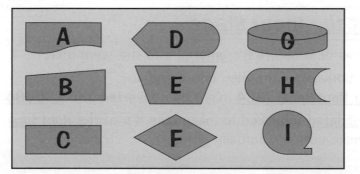

13) Which would be the correct symbol for each of the following events?
    a) Displaying a screen prompt to log on
    b) Keying in your user name
    c) The computer checking that your user name is on its list
    d) Making a hard copy of a document

14) Explain how parallel implementation is different from direct implementation.

15) Explain how phased implementation is different from parallel implementation.

16) Give one benefit and one problem of each type of implementation.

17) What are the three types of test data needed? Give an example for each if testing the validation of data entries for the field "Day of month born".

18) What is the difference between system testing and acceptance testing?

19) List three different types of user documentation — and explain when each one should be used.

20) What is the difference between monitoring and evaluation?

21) Describe two occasions when the technical documentation of a system will be needed.

Information and Data

You already know that computers are machines for <u>processing data</u>.
But for that to make complete sense, you need to know <u>exactly</u> what data is. Read on, my friend.

Data has No Meaning

Data is <u>information</u> that has <u>no meaning</u>. For example, take the number 120987.
The number could mean <u>absolutely anything</u>. It could be a birthday, an amount of money,
a phone number, or about a billion other things. But one thing it <u>isn't</u> is information.

Data only becomes information when you know the <u>context</u> of the data.

> Information = Data + Meaning

<u>Computers</u> are machines that <u>process data</u>.
But they're <u>stupid</u> — they don't understand the data they process.

Learn the Input, Process, Output Cycle

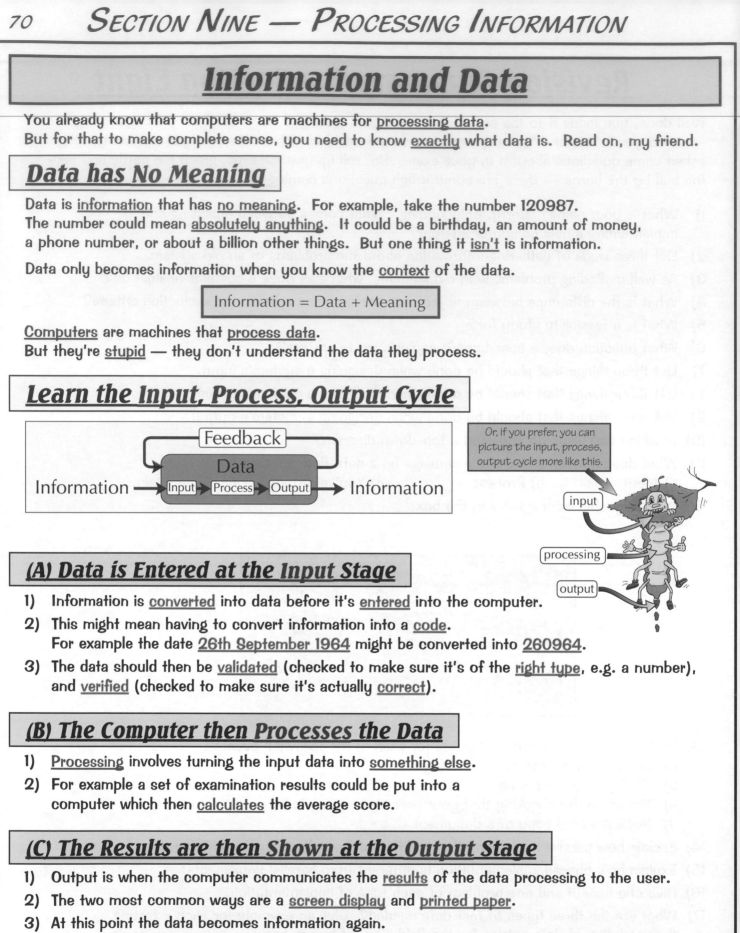

Or, if you prefer, you can picture the input, process, output cycle more like this.

input
processing
output

(A) Data is Entered at the Input Stage

1) Information is <u>converted</u> into data before it's <u>entered</u> into the computer.

2) This might mean having to convert information into a <u>code</u>.
For example the date <u>26th September 1964</u> might be converted into <u>260964</u>.

3) The data should then be <u>validated</u> (checked to make sure it's of the <u>right type</u>, e.g. a number),
and <u>verified</u> (checked to make sure it's actually <u>correct</u>).

(B) The Computer then Processes the Data

1) <u>Processing</u> involves turning the input data into <u>something else</u>.

2) For example a set of examination results could be put into a
computer which then <u>calculates</u> the average score.

(C) The Results are then Shown at the Output Stage

1) Output is when the computer communicates the <u>results</u> of the data processing to the user.

2) The two most common ways are a <u>screen display</u> and <u>printed paper</u>.

3) At this point the data becomes information again.

4) The information obtained at this stage might then be used as <u>feedback</u> to <u>input more data</u>.
This turns the system into a <u>cycle</u>.

This is all just data-day stuff...

If you get a computer to process incorrect data, the results will be meaningless. This is called
<u>Garbage In, Garbage Out (GIGO)</u>. Some people call this 'computer error', but they're wrong — it's
human error. Computers hardly ever make mistakes. They just do what they're <u>programmed</u> to do.

Searching for Information

We can access <u>more useless information</u> now than at any time in history. That's progress.

We Live in an Information Age...

1) Even now, a lot of our information comes from fairly <u>traditional</u> sources — for example, newspapers, magazines, books, maps, conversations... and so on and so on.

2) But digital technology means we can now <u>process</u> and <u>store</u> data more easily and cheaply than ever before. <u>Communications</u> technology has also improved massively over the last decades. The result is that <u>more information</u> is now communicated to <u>more people</u> than ever before.

3) For example, we now have CDs and DVD-ROMs (so cheap that newspapers often give them away), <u>text messages</u>, and probably most importantly, the <u>Internet</u>.

4) The Internet means we now have access to:
   - <u>blogs</u> (short for "web logs") — these are a bit like "online diaries".
   - <u>podcasts</u> — downloadable <u>media files</u> that are often <u>syndicated</u> (made available for download on other sites). People can <u>subscribe</u> to receive new "episodes" as they're released.
   - <u>e-books</u> — downloadable from the Internet and read on <u>computers</u> or <u>electronic readers</u>.
   - <u>wikis</u> — <u>collaborative websites</u> that can be edited using just a normal <u>web-browser</u>.
   - <u>online databases</u> — accessible from <u>any</u> computer connected to the Internet.

There's more about collaborative working on page 82.

...but a Lot of That Information is Useless Junk

One word of warning... "<u>quality control</u>" on the Internet isn't everything it could be.

1) <u>Not everything</u> on the Internet is <u>true</u>... but it's often hard to tell the <u>good</u> stuff from the <u>bad</u>.

2) There's also the problem of <u>security</u>. Information can be accessed <u>illegally</u> and so potentially changed. Also, any data you download may bring with it <u>unwanted</u> stuff like viruses.

3) And security problems don't just affect businesses and organisations. Even information <u>you</u> send is vulnerable (e.g. your address or credit card details)... so beware.

DO CRAB to Help Find the Information Gems

Following this "<u>DO CRAB</u>" advice means you're more likely to find <u>useful info</u> than junk.

DATE <u>When</u> was the information put on the Internet? (It could be <u>out of date</u>.)

Oh dear I can't actually think of anything for "O".

CLEAR <u>Don't</u> use information you <u>don't understand</u> — you might get the wrong end of the stick.

RELEVANT <u>Make sure</u> the information is <u>relevant</u> to your needs.

AUTHORS <u>Who</u> wrote the information? Would you expect them to be experts on the subject? (E.g. I might not totally believe an essay on quantum physics written by the Chuckle Brothers. Or at least... I'd double check that they <u>had</u> actually studied quantum physics.)

Remember...

BIAS Ask whether the authors are definitely <u>objective</u>. Or could they be <u>biased</u> for some reason? (E.g., a business might exaggerate the usefulness of one of its products.)

At night, crabs wail like banshees... (a fact I found on www.amazingbutfalse.com)

Data is vulnerable when it's <u>stored</u> (e.g. if it's stored on a computer connected to a network). And it's especially vulnerable while it's being <u>transmitted</u> from one place to another. So take care of your data, and don't let baddies get it. Okay, lecture over. Now get on and <u>learn</u> this stuff.

Data Collection

Data capture is the way that information's first gathered and put on a computer system. It's the input part of the 'input — process — output' cycle.

Data Capture turns Information into Data

Data capture is sometimes called data collection. It's a two-part process.

1) The information has to be obtained.
2) The data has to be entered onto the computer using an input device.

First you have to Catch your Rabbit...

1) MANUAL METHODS of capturing data involve a person — usually to key in information that someone else has supplied on a paper-based data-capture form or questionnaire.

2) AUTOMATIC METHODS of data capture don't require a person to key in data supplied by someone else. All sorts of automatic data capture methods exist these days, such as...

- ONLINE FORMS — users can type information into a form on a website. This info can then be used to automatically update a database or place an order, for example.
- CARD READERS — credit card numbers are read automatically, from either a microchip (as in "Chip and PIN") on the front of the card or the magnetic stripe on the back.
- BAR CODE READERS — e.g. in supermarkets, product codes can be quickly scanned.
- VOICE RECOGNITION devices — like the ones used in security entry systems.
- BIOMETRICS — like when a scanner reads the fingerprint info stored on a passport (which can then be checked against a person's actual fingerprint to check that the passport is really theirs).
- RFID TAGS — contain information that can be read by radio receivers. They're often found in vehicles (to automatically pay tolls for tunnels, bridges and so on) or products (so shops and delivery companies can track individual items).
- OMR DEVICES (Optical Mark Recognition — see p4). Forms sometimes need to be filled in by making marks in particular places. These marks are then read using a scanner. Examples include computerised school registers and multiple-choice answer sheets.

> 21. You are driving along the motorway and you hit a rabbit. Do you:
> A: Stop and walk back to pick it up.
> B: Continue driving.
> C: Pull onto the hard shoulder and ring the vet.
> D: Drive over it a few times, just to make sure.
>
> A B C D
> ☐ ☐ ☐ ☐

Each Method has its Advantages

AUTOMATIC DATA CAPTURE SYSTEMS
Faster and more accurate than manual systems. Humans don't have to be present — so it's useful in dangerous/inaccessible places (e.g. nuclear reactors).

MANUAL DATA CAPTURE SYSTEMS
Cheaper — less hardware and software needed, so the system will be less expensive.

I smell carrots a cookin' and where there's carrots, there's wabbits...

OK, loads of words, but not really that much to learn. Just concentrate on learning one example each of manual and automatic data capture. Then for each example check you can explain both why that method's good, and why the other methods wouldn't be so good.

Checking Data

OK, here are the two main methods of making sure that the data entered is <u>accurate</u>...

Data Validation Checks the Data is of the Correct Type

Data validation checks that the data is of the <u>right type</u> (e.g. percentages should be numbers from 0 to 100). Validation can be performed automatically by the computer whilst data is entered.

1) **RANGE CHECK:** This checks that the data is within a <u>specified range</u>. For example, a person's month of birth should be a number between 1 and 12.

2) **PRESENCE CHECK:** This <u>makes sure</u> that important information has actually been <u>entered</u>. For example, a customer record might have to contain their date of birth, so the software won't allow the date of birth field to be left empty.

3) **CHECK DIGIT:** This checks that <u>numerical</u> data has been entered <u>accurately</u>. The final digit of a number is determined by a <u>formula</u> that uses all the previous digits. So if the number's been entered incorrectly, the check digit will be wrong. A good example is the <u>ISBN</u> number on a book — the last digit is a check digit.

The team gave 120%

Validation error.

4) **DATA TYPE CHECK:** This checks that <u>text</u> hasn't been put where <u>numbers</u> are needed, for example.

5) **LOOK-UP LISTS:** These allow the user to enter just the first few characters of an entry. The computer then presents a list of all "legal" entries that start with those characters, and the user can select one.

6) **LENGTH CHECK:** This makes sure that the entry is the <u>right length</u>. For example, a <u>date of birth</u> has to be exactly 8 digits long (DDMMYYYY).

The main benefit of data validation is that it's automatic — so it is quick and easy to spot errors.

Data Verification Ensures the Data is Accurate

Data verification is different — it means making sure the data which has been input is <u>the same</u> as the original data. There are two main verification techniques.

1) **PROOF-READING** is when a <u>person</u> reads the data that has been entered onto the system and <u>compares</u> it with the original. Any incorrectly entered data will be edited.

2) **DOUBLE-ENTRY** is when the data is <u>entered twice</u> by two different people. The computer then compares the two versions. Any errors found are then corrected.

Pick a number. Any whole number. Between 2 and 3.

Validation and Verification Both have their Problems

Sadly, nothing's perfect and these checks are no exception — they both have their problems.

Problems with Data Validation	Problems with Data Verification
1) Any <u>problems</u> with the validation <u>program</u> could mean mistakes are allowed.	1) Double-entry is <u>time consuming</u> — and so it can be very <u>expensive</u>.
2) It <u>only</u> makes sure that the data is the <u>right type</u> — <u>not</u> that it is accurate.	2) Proof-reading is also time consuming — and doesn't eliminate <u>human error</u>.

Presence check — what I do every Christmas...

<u>Validation</u>, <u>verification</u> — two fun new ways to say '<u>checking</u>'. The main thing here is to know the <u>difference</u> between them and the <u>pros and cons</u> of each method. It might help to draw a table...

IKBS and Expert Systems

Expert systems sound pretty exciting. But IKBS sounds as dull as any other 4-letter acronym.

Expert Systems Ask a Series of Questions

1) Information Knowledge-Based Systems (IKBS) are also known as Expert systems.

2) They're intended to model the knowledge of a human expert — meaning that the expert system should be able to replace the human.

3) They contain a 'knowledge bank' of data about a particular subject, as well as a set of instructions for processing the knowledge.

4) The idea is that the computer asks the user a series of questions, with the answer to each question helping to determine what the next question should be. Eventually the computer has enough information to suggest a solution to the problem.

5) Expert systems can be used to give advice about illnesses that match certain symptoms, or advice on tax/welfare benefits etc.

Expert Systems Can Help Solve Technical Problems

Some computer operating systems use expert systems to help sort out technical difficulties.

1) The expert system asks a question, which the user answers.

2) Depending on the answer, the expert system might suggest a possible fix to the problem. If it does, hooray. If not, the system asks another question.

3) The system asks a series of questions and can suggest a series of possible fixes. The expert system helps find the correct solution as quickly as possible without having to try them all.

The Ups

1) Common problems can be solved relatively quickly.

2) It's efficient — one expert system can be used in many different places to solve loads of different problems at the same time.

3) Even quite obscure problems can often be fixed — if the "knowledge bank" and the supply of questions are detailed enough.

4) The knowledge bank and questions can easily be updated so that more problems can be solved.

The Downs

1) It needs the user to have a certain amount of technical knowledge — it might not work if the person with the problem knows absolutely nothing about computers (they might not be able to answer the questions, or try the suggested fixes).

2) Some people might prefer to talk to a human to solve the problem.

3) It's only as good as the knowledge and questions that have been programmed into it, and so might not be able to fix all problems.

Sadly, you can't take an expert system into your ICT exam...

Well... not an automated one, anyway — you're going to be totally reliant on the expert system in your brain. So update the knowledge bank by revising this page very very carefully. And then test yourself by writing down all you can remember. Have another go if you get anything wrong.

Revision Summary for Section Nine

Well that's another section over and done with — not. You know the score by now — you've read the stuff, you think you've learnt it — but have you really? Get all these questions right first time and you can call yourself a genius. Get some wrong and you can jolly well go back and learn the stuff properly.

1) What's the difference between data and information?

2) Describe the input–process–output cycle of data processing.

3) Describe what's meant by the following:
   a) a blog
   b) a podcast
   c) syndication
   d) e-book
   e) wiki

4) Why should you be careful about believing everything you read on the Internet?

5) How can you tell a reliable source of information on the Internet from a dodgy one?

6) What is meant by data capture? What two things does it involve?

7) What's the difference between automatic and manual data capture? Give two examples of each.

8) Give one advantage each of manual and automatic data capture systems.

9) How should instructions be written on a data capture form?
   a) Using complex syntax and vocabulary to communicate elementary linguistic structures.
   b) In plain English.
   c) In binary.

10) What's the difference between data validation and data verification?

11) Explain any four methods of data validation.

12) Explain any two methods of data verification.

13) Describe two problems each with data validation and data verification.

14) What does IKBS stand for?

15) What does an expert system do? How does it work?

16) Give three possible uses for an expert system.

17) Give four advantages and two disadvantages of an expert system.

18) What comes after Section Nine?

Computers and the Law

Computers are used to store and process important data — so there are laws to control their use.

The Data Protection Act Controls the Use of Personal Data

1) The Data Protection Act was introduced in the UK in 1984. It gives rights to data subjects (i.e. people who have data about them stored on computer systems). The Act was updated in 1998 to take the increasing use of computers, and changes in European Union law, into account.

2) The Act mainly consists of eight data protection principles — summarised here:

3) The law requires that most organisations that plan to retain data register with the government.

4) It also entitles data subjects to see the personal data about them that's held by an organisation. If an organisation breaks the law, they can be fined and made to pay compensation to the data subject.

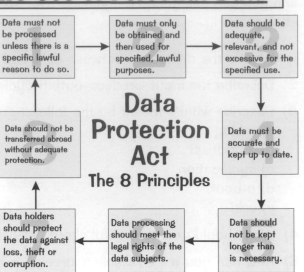

Data must not be processed unless there is a specific lawful reason to do so.

Data must only be obtained and then used for specified, lawful purposes.

Data should be adequate, relevant, and not excessive for the specified use.

Data Protection Act
The 8 Principles

Data should not be transferred abroad without adequate protection.

Data must be accurate and kept up to date.

Data holders should protect the data against loss, theft or corruption.

Data processing should meet the legal rights of the data subjects.

Data should not be kept longer than is necessary.

5) However, some data is exempt from access by data subjects. This includes data that might:

- affect a criminal investigation
- affect the outcome of a court case

- affect a tax assessment
- identify another person (unless that other person has given their consent)

The Personal Data Guardianship Code is for Data Handlers

1) The Personal Data Guardianship Code was created to help people follow the Data Protection Act.

2) It suggests that organisations have one senior person who is responsible for data handling.

3) The responsible person has five main duties (the principles of the code):

1) Accountability: they're responsible for making sure that personal data is handled appropriately.

2) Visibility: they must state how the data is going to be used, and if it's being passed on to third parties.

3) Consent: they must get the consent of the data subject before accessing or sharing their personal data.

4) Access: they must make sure that personal data is secure from people who shouldn't be able to see it, both inside and outside of the organisation.

5) Stewardship: they must make sure that the amount of data accessed is not excessive, and that it's securely deleted when it's not needed any more.

The Computer Misuse Act Prevents Illegal Access to Files

This law was introduced in 1990 to cope with the problems of computer hackers and viruses. The Act made the following three things illegal:

1) Unauthorised access to computer material (e.g. hacking). This includes viewing parts of a network you're not permitted to see, and the illegal copying of programs — software piracy.

2) Gaining unauthorised access to a computer to carry out serious crimes like fraud and blackmail.

3) Unauthorised changing of computer files — including planting viruses, and deleting files.

If convicted, the offender can face an unlimited fine and a five-year prison sentence.

I turned my PC into a fish tank — that's computer misuse...

It's nice to know that these laws and guidelines exist. It's a bit of a shame that you need to know about each one in some detail... make sure you know their full names and what they do.

Hardware and Data Security

Now you know the legal stuff, it's time to find out about <u>protecting</u> computer hardware and data.

Physical Security Protects the Hardware

Hardware is <u>expensive</u> — follow these 7 rules to keep it safe.

1) **Serial numbers** — Keep a record of all <u>serial numbers</u>, and mark the organisation's name and postcode on all equipment — this helps police to identify stolen property.

2) **Alarms** — Computer rooms should be protected by <u>burglar alarms</u>.

3) **Fire protection** — Use fireproof doors and smoke alarms. Also, automatic <u>gas-flooding systems</u> could be used to put out any fires to prevent water damaging the equipment.

4) **Lock** windows and doors to <u>prevent access</u>.

5) **Avoid** putting computers on the <u>ground floor</u> of buildings, where they can be easily seen from outside.

6) **Blinds** or curtains should be <u>closed</u> at night, and monitors should be <u>switched off</u>, so the computers are less visible.

7) **Surveillance** — security cameras can be installed to <u>put off</u> would-be thieves, or to help <u>identify</u> anyone who has stolen something.

Access Security Limits a Person's Use of the Network

1) All <u>authorised users</u> should be given <u>user names</u> and create their own <u>passwords</u>. This will limit <u>unauthorised access</u> to the network.

2) Individual users can be assigned <u>access rights</u>. For example, network managers can be given access to the software that controls how the network is run, while other users can be <u>limited</u> to <u>certain types</u> of <u>application software</u> such as word processors.

3) A <u>firewall increases</u> the protection of a network from <u>external threats</u> (like hackers). They offer some security, but <u>can't</u> provide total protection.

4) <u>Intrusion detection</u> flags up attempts to hack into a network <u>as they happen</u>. Some intrusion detectors <u>automatically limit</u> network access when they think a hack is taking place.

Be Careful with your Data when Using the Internet

1) <u>Phishing</u> is when a not-so-nice person sends you an <u>e-mail</u>, pretending to be from your bank or another organisation that holds your <u>personal details</u>.

2) You're usually asked to enter your <u>personal details</u> on a website linked to in the email.

3) The website often looks like a <u>real website</u> — it might <u>fool people</u> into believing it's the real deal.

4) The not-so-nice person hopes you'll put in your details so they can <u>steal your identity</u>.

5) A common <u>policy</u> of banks and other organisations is that they'll <u>never ask</u> for your details in an <u>email</u> (or over the phone) — so you can just <u>delete</u> e-mails that do ask for this info.

6) Banks have a <u>number of procedures</u> to <u>protect</u> your data when you're doing <u>online banking</u>.

7) Many require accounts to have <u>multiple passwords</u> and <u>secret answers</u>.

8) Some banks send out <u>card readers</u> to their customers — like the Chip & PIN devices in shops.

Gullible web users are phishermen's friends...

This page <u>isn't</u> too difficult, and you've probably heard of most of this <u>security</u> stuff before. Make sure you understand what <u>phishing</u> is — it could come in handy for your exam, and in <u>real life</u> too.

Health and Safety Issues

Computers weren't originally designed to be used all day. Make sure you know about the health and safety risks of continuous computer use and what can be done to reduce them.

Computer Use can Cause Three Main Health Problems...

There are three main problems — connected either with poor design of the equipment, or from not using the equipment properly. In each case the risk is small, but the effects can be serious.

1) Repetitive strain injury (RSI) is the general term for aches, pains and muscle or tendon damage resulting from overuse of a keyboard or mouse. Many medical conditions have been linked to RSI, such as carpal tunnel syndrome which causes finger pain and numbness.

2) Spending too long in front of a monitor can cause eye strain and headaches. Screen glare and poor-quality images on older monitors can make it hard for the eyes to focus properly.

3) Circulation, fitness and back problems might result from sitting all day in front of a computer rather than walking around. This is more of a long-term health problem.

...Which Have Three Main Solutions

1) Take regular breaks from computer work. Looking away from the screen, walking around and exercising your fingers and hands can also help to reduce the health risks.

> **AS A GENERAL RULE**
> 1) Your forearms should be roughly horizontal.
> 2) Your eyes should be level with the top of the monitor.

2) Use the correct equipment. You should have:

   a) a proper computer chair with backrest,

   b) an ergonomically-designed keyboard that makes it easier to touch-type without straining fingers,

   c) good background lighting and a screen filter to reduce monitor glare.

3) Arrange equipment properly. Adjust the chair and monitor to find the most comfortable position.

Employers Need to Follow the Law

The main law covering computer use at work is the Health and Safety (Display Screen Equipment) Regulations 1992. The law says that employers need to do five main things:

1) **ANALYSE WORKSTATIONS, AND ASSESS AND REDUCE RISKS:** Employers need to check that computer equipment (and the area around it) is safe, e.g. there are no overloaded sockets, no trailing wires and malfunctioning equipment is replaced.

2) **ENSURE WORKSTATIONS MEET MINIMUM REQUIREMENTS:** Lighting needs to be correct, e.g. enough ambient light, and direct sunlight blocked using blinds. Workstations shouldn't be at an extreme temperature, i.e. too hot or too cold — air conditioning can control this.

3) **PLAN WORK SO THERE ARE BREAKS OR CHANGES OF ACTIVITY:** Employers mustn't expect workers to work at a computer all day. They must provide regular breaks or allow them to do non-computer work.

4) **PROVIDE FREE EYE-TESTS:** to all staff who regularly use monitors as part of their job.

5) **PROVIDE HEALTH AND SAFETY TRAINING AND INFORMATION:** So employees can take action themselves to reduce the health risks, e.g. no eating or drinking at desks — this improves hygiene.

Take an eye test — make sure you've got no more than two...

But surely no one expected sitting down all day to be as healthy as running around in the fresh air... Cover the page, make a table with one column for problems and another for solutions, then fill it in.

Computers and the Workplace

All these fancy computers have had quite a <u>big impact</u> on the world of business, and guess what — you need to know all about it. Enjoyment commences in 5, 4, 3, 2, 1...

ICT has Replaced Some Jobs but Created Others

1) Computers have completely <u>replaced</u> humans in performing some jobs, and <u>reduced</u> the number of people needed to do others.

2) These have mainly been <u>repetitive jobs</u>, or those that involve applying rules in a <u>logical way</u> — this is what computers do best.

3) However, computers aren't that good at <u>social skills</u> — so jobs that need a <u>human touch</u> won't be taken over by computers for a while yet.

4) Computers and technology help to <u>create</u> jobs too — there are jobs and industries that only exist at all because of computers.

JOBS REPLACED BY COMPUTERS

1) <u>Manual jobs</u> replaced by <u>robots</u>, e.g. some car-assembly jobs.

2) Many <u>office jobs</u> replaced by <u>computers</u>, e.g. many accountancy/finance tasks can be performed by computers.

INDUSTRIES CREATED BY COMPUTERS

1) <u>Network</u> management.
2) <u>Data</u> management.
3) <u>Systems</u> analysis and management.
4) <u>Hardware</u> and <u>software</u> manufacturing.

ICT Enables Completely New Ways of Working

Here are a few <u>examples</u> of how ICT has changed the workplace:

1) <u>Automated stock control</u> is the process of managing stock levels (e.g. in a shop) <u>without</u> human input.

2) When an item is <u>sold</u>, the sale information is passed on to a stock-control system that monitors stock levels.

3) If the number of any item in stock has fallen <u>below a certain level</u>, the system will <u>automatically</u> order more.

Your stock control is terrible!

1) In recent years it has become increasingly popular for people to shop on the <u>Internet</u> (<u>e-commerce</u>), rather than in actual shops.

2) This has reduced the need for some businesses to have a '<u>high-street presence</u>' — they can sell just as much but without the <u>costs</u> of renting and running a building.

1) <u>Just-in-Time</u> (JIT) stock control is often used by manufacturers now.

2) The <u>Just-in-Time</u> method aims to keep stock levels to the <u>bare minimum</u> — ideally zero. Stock is <u>used immediately</u> as it arrives, so there's no cost for <u>storing</u> it.

3) JIT wouldn't be possible without excellent <u>communications</u> and constant monitoring of stock levels and rates of usage — things computers and improvements in ICT have made much easier.

My computer has social skills — the social skills of a brick...

Unfortunately you're <u>not allowed</u> to employ a computer to sit your exams for you. But don't worry, the good <u>old fashioned method</u> of learning this page until you know it backwards will see you right.

Computers and the Workplace

All of these technological advances have helped the world become a smaller place — not literally, mind, but you can communicate with people thousands of miles away as if they were right next to you.

Globalisation has been Partly Caused by ICT

1) Globalisation is the process of all the world's systems and cultures becoming more integrated — it's the whole world coming together like a single community.

2) This has become possible because of developments in communications (and transport) technology.

3) Important developments include e-mail, the Internet, mobile phones, as well as technology to transfer more information more quickly.

4) This allows businesses to operate all over the world. For example, a company can have its offices in one country and easily communicate with manufacturing plants and markets on the other side of the world — nowadays people don't need face-to-face meetings in order to communicate effectively.

A company that operates in more than one country is called a multinational corporation (MNC).

5) Some industries have been completely transformed. For example, stock markets (where shares in companies are bought and sold) used to involve people making deals face to face with other people. Nowadays everything is done on computers — you can buy shares in a foreign company without leaving your seat.

Emerging Technologies are Changing Things for the Future

New technologies have always had a big effect on businesses — e.g. steam engines and the telephone were new technologies once. More recently, computers and the Internet changed things forever. "Emerging technologies" could transform businesses in the future. Here are a few examples:

Biometrics: this is all about identifying a person from their bodily features — e.g. their fingerprints, irises (the coloured bit in your eyes) or face. Biometric data is generally unique to an individual, so it's a good way of making sure someone is who they say they are — this means biometrics are useful for things like ID cards, passports, and logging on to computers.

3D printing: this is when three-dimensional objects are made by printing layers of material on top of each other. It's useful for making prototypes of products quickly and cheaply. In the olden days (a few years ago) the only way to get a prototype was by using skilled people to make models — 3D printing will mean this process is as easily done by an office worker as an engineer.

Computer-assisted translation: before computers, translations were done by skilled linguists. Nowadays, computer-assisted translation allows anyone to translate more or less anything.

Computer assisted translation isn't 100% accurate yet, but it keeps getting better.

New technologies emerge all the time, and the effects on business and people's everyday lives can be hard to predict.

The world might be getting smaller — but your revision isn't...

Globalisation is a funny word that's bandied about a lot, but make sure you understand what it means and why ICT is helping to increase it. Then learn the rest of the page as a treat...

Computers and People

So, if computers have an impact on <u>businesses</u>, you'd expect them to have an impact on the <u>people</u> working for the businesses too. Well expected. This page is all about that, so have a gander...

ICT enables Flexible Working

1) Rather than travel to an office, Internet technology makes it possible for employees to <u>telework</u> (i.e. work from home), <u>uploading</u> and <u>downloading</u> work as necessary. It has <u>advantages</u> and <u>disadvantages</u>:

> Teleworking is useful for people doing collaborative work (see page 82).

Advantages	Disadvantages
<u>Less time</u> is spent on <u>commuting</u>. It means you can spend <u>more time</u> on doing your work (or relaxing). It also cuts down on <u>travel costs</u>.	You <u>won't</u> have as much <u>face-to-face contact</u> with your colleagues, so it's easy to feel isolated. Sometimes it's easier to <u>communicate</u> with people in person (plus it's always nice to have a <u>chat</u> with someone).
<u>Working conditions</u> can be <u>tailored</u> in your own home. You can have the <u>radio</u> on, open a <u>window</u>, eat <u>radishes</u> — anything to make you <u>more comfortable</u> while you work.	You might get <u>distracted</u> at home, e.g. you could nip to the <u>shops</u>, do the <u>washing up</u>, watch a <u>film</u>... and there'll be no one to <u>tell</u> you to get on with your work.

2) <u>Mobile computing</u> has allowed people to work <u>on the move</u> — they're not tied down to a desk in an office. Modern mobile computers, e.g. laptops and PDAs, can be as <u>powerful</u> as desktop computers, although their <u>battery life</u> can restrict just how mobile they actually are.

3) <u>Hot-desking</u> is another buzzword that's all about flexible working — employees sit at <u>any free desk</u> in an office, rather than having their own designated place. It could be in one of their <u>employer's offices</u>, or in a <u>work-centre</u> shared by people who work for different organisations.

This is made possible because many employees <u>don't</u> need to use <u>physical objects</u> (e.g. tools or books) to carry out their jobs — they just need <u>access</u> to computer files (e.g. software or data stored on a network).

ICT can Increase Job Satisfaction but it Requires Training

1) Advances in ICT have made it much <u>easier</u> for workers to carry out tasks that in the past would have been <u>too specialised</u> to do themselves. For example, thanks to 3D printing (see p80), designers can actually create scale models of their designs. And small-business owners can create professional-looking brochures to show their products.

2) This has increased <u>productivity</u> (which is good for the business) and improved <u>job satisfaction</u> (which is good for workers).

3) However, in order to use all this technology <u>effectively</u>, people have to be <u>trained</u> — which can cost a business <u>time</u> and <u>money</u>.

4) And since technology <u>improves</u> all the time, keeping up to date with the latest developments can be <u>expensive</u> — there's the obvious cost of <u>buying</u> the technology, but there's also the cost of <u>retraining</u> people.

Teleworking? Yep, thanks very much — it's HD ready, too...

All this talk of <u>flexible working</u> is making me want to do a huge <u>stretch</u>. I love stretching — it's such a nice thing to do. Almost as nice as <u>revising</u> a page on the effects that ICT has had on people...

Collaborative Working

If you find revising a bit <u>lonely</u> then the next two pages have been created with you in mind — they are all about <u>working with other people</u>. Or maybe they're mocking you, because you're all alone...

Collaborative Working is Basically Team Work

1) Collaborative working is where people <u>work together</u> to reach a <u>common goal</u>.

2) The people could be <u>individuals</u>, part of an official <u>group</u> or <u>team</u> within a business, a whole <u>organisation</u>, or even entire <u>countries</u>.

3) Collaboration is often a <u>recursive process</u> (e.g. if Abe and Bob are working on the same document, then Abe might do a little bit of work, then Bob might do something to it, then Abe does a bit more, and so on).

A Group Plan can Reduce Conflict and Increase Consistency

1) Lots of people working together always has the <u>potential for disaster</u> — everyone has their <u>own opinion</u> on how to do something, which can cause <u>conflicts</u>.

2) People working on a project should have a <u>plan</u> of the best way to achieve the <u>common goal</u> — it should take everyone's opinion into <u>account</u> (but not everyone will think it's <u>perfect</u>).

3) As work on the project begins, <u>individuals</u> should be <u>checking</u> that their work <u>follows</u> the plan.

4) <u>One part</u> of the plan might be a description of the <u>layout</u> for any documents produced during the project, e.g. reports and presentations — this is the <u>house style</u>.

5) House styles are <u>good</u> for collaborative work, otherwise the finished project could be a bit of a dog's breakfast — an ugly mix of clashing colours and fonts.

Project Management is Vital to Collaborative Working

1) <u>Project management</u> is all about <u>making sure</u> a project is completed on time, on budget, and that it meets the required objectives.

2) Balancing all of these things is <u>not easy</u> — they may <u>change</u> after the project has been started, e.g. it might need to be completed in three weeks not five, or the project might have to solve world hunger as well as the original objective of world peace.

3) All of the <u>work</u> towards a project has to be <u>scheduled</u> — each bit must be planned to take place at a certain time. The <u>fewer unknowns</u> there are about a project, the <u>easier</u> it is to <u>manage</u>.

4) <u>Each individual</u> working on a project has to be aware that their <u>key role</u> is to finish their work by the given <u>deadline</u>. If they don't, they'll <u>slow down</u> the project or even <u>prevent</u> it from achieving its objectives.

Oh, and if you miss your deadline you'll be electrocuted.

Sorry, what?

Nothing...

5) <u>Good communication</u> between individuals in the collaboration is also <u>vital</u> — people should be <u>aware</u> of other people's <u>work schedules</u>, and <u>meetings</u> could be <u>synchronised</u> (happen at the same time), so that more than one thing can be discussed and <u>more people's opinions</u> can be heard.

Let's work together and think of something funny to go here...

All this collaborative working stuff <u>seems obvious</u>, but don't fall into the <u>trap</u> of assuming you know it all. You need to be able to <u>describe</u> things like group plans and project management.

Collaborative Working and Software

So, you're now the resident expert on collaborative working. But I reckon it's about time you knew about when it's used and the stuff that can help make the whole collaborative thing a lot easier...

Collaboration Happens in Different Situations

1) An obvious place for collaboration is in businesses — it can be more efficient than people working on their own (as long as communication is good), which saves businesses time and money.

2) It's also found in education — students can work together to achieve a goal, e.g. completing a homework project. It helps them to develop their communication and organisation skills.

3) Many leisure activities involve collaboration. For example, online games sometimes require players to work together to achieve their objectives.

Software can Make Collaborative Work Easier

Shared workspaces are areas on the Web used for storing things like documents, to-do lists and calendars. Members of a collaboration can log on to the workspace to view and edit documents, add things to the calendar and so on. It's a bit like a shared computer that exists on the Web.

Workflow is basically the sequence of steps something has to go through before it's finished. Some software can automate these steps, e.g. after a document has been edited, it's automatically sent to someone to proofread it.

Project management tools help to plan a project efficiently, e.g. schedule tasks, assign people to complete those tasks and show how much of a project has been completed.

Communication tools that help collaborative work include VoIP (Voice over Internet Protocol — transmitting speech via the internet), instant messaging, telephones, e-mail... I could go on. You might not be too familiar with teleconferencing though...

Teleconferencing Links People in Different Places

1) Teleconferencing uses ICT to connect people in different locations using sound and/or video.

2) Locations are connected by a telecommunications system (e.g. a phone line, the Internet, or a satellite link) so that several people can communicate as though they're in the same room.

3) There are two main types of teleconferencing:

AUDIO CONFERENCING allows oral communication only.
- Each person has a microphone to talk into, and a speaker that outputs what other people are saying.
- Audio conferences can be held using fairly basic telephones, so it's not too expensive.
- On the downside, you can't see people's body language, so messages are easier to misunderstand.

VIDEO CONFERENCING allows oral and visual communication.
- It uses speakers, microphones, video cameras and monitors to transmit sound and images.
- You can see people during the meeting, so it's more human and personal.
- But the equipment is more expensive than normal telephones.

4) Teleconferencing saves time and money on travelling to a meeting place — people can hold meetings without leaving their offices.

5) But teleconferencing is not perfect — there's always the risk of technical failure — if the machinery breaks down, then the meeting's over.

6) There can also be delays as messages are transmitted — this can make conversation difficult.

A telly conference is the place to be for broadcasting news...

I've spoiled you with another easy-ish page, so return the favour and make sure you get all of this lodged in your brain. Don't forget about the advantages and disadvantages of teleconferencing.

Collaborative Working — Sharing Info

All this collaborative working isn't much use if the different parts of a project aren't brought together. Fortunately the Internet has made sharing stuff much easier, but there are things to be aware of...

Naming Conventions and Version Control are Important

1) To manage files effectively, filenames and different versions of files need to be controlled.

2) Naming conventions for files mean everyone on a project names documents the same way. It avoids confusion when lots of people are working with similar files. A naming convention might include the following:

> - File description — a brief explanation of what the file contains.
> - Date of creation — in a specific format e.g. YYYY-MM-DD.
> - No spaces or special characters — these can cause errors, or make the filename look weird, e.g. spaces are converted to '%20' by web browsers.

You've got to make sure that everyone is using the same naming convention and version control method — otherwise it's all pointless...

3) Version control helps if you have lots of files that are different versions of the same thing.

4) One way of distinguishing between versions is to put a lowercase 'v' (for 'version') and a number at the end of the filename — start at 1 and go upwards. So if someone wants to open the most recent version they just look for the highest number.

Data needs to be Securely Accessed and Transferred

1) With some collaborative work there may be documents that should only be accessed or edited by certain people, e.g. personal information or results data.

2) Some operating systems let you change the access rights of files so you can control what people can and can't do with them — this kind of security helps to reduce accidents and increase confidentiality.

3) The transfer of data also needs to be done securely — especially when using the Internet.

4) Loads of files are transferred using the Internet — they're uploaded to a file server (see page 51), and someone else can download them at a later time.

5) User names, passwords and encryption (converting the data into a code) help to protect the data as it's being transferred — the chances of a thief being able to read it are reduced.

6) Files can also be transferred physically, e.g. on a USB drive or a DVD. Password-protecting or encrypting them can prevent the files from being used if they fall into the wrong hands.

Compressing Files can Reduce Transfer Times

1) The bigger a file's size, the longer it takes to transfer it to another computer.

2) File-compression software can compress (zip) files using algorithms, which makes transferring them quicker. The programs can also decompress (unzip) zipped files, so they have the same file size as the original files.

3) A file's data isn't changed when it's zipped up — it's just stored in a different way. It's a bit like scrunching up a sponge — it gets smaller, but it'll pop back to how it was when you let it go.

Meet my older brother — 1984-06-23_Offspring_Male_v1...

Naming conventions and version control sound really geeky, but they're both extremely useful when it comes to file management. The same thing goes for passwords, encryption and file compression.

Online Behaviour

Something weird's just happened — I have become your <u>mother</u>. Don't be alarmed, I'm just here to give you some <u>words of wisdom</u> about the online kingdom. Yes, it's boring — but it's <u>important</u>.

The Internet is Great — but is Not Without Problems

The beauty of the Internet is that it lets you access <u>almost everything</u> you could ever want. But its <u>simplicity</u> and <u>global scale</u> has allowed people to use it for <u>evil</u>...

Getting your mitts on things like <u>programs</u>, <u>music</u>, and <u>films</u> is incredibly <u>easy</u> thanks to the Internet — a <u>lot</u> of people download things without a second thought. But unless the person or organisation that owns the stuff gives <u>permission</u> to download it, it's <u>illegal</u>. <u>Online theft</u> is a <u>crime</u>, as much as it is in the 'real world'.

Information on the Web <u>isn't always reliable</u>. People can either accidentally or intentionally upload <u>incorrect information</u>, which can then be passed quickly around the <u>world</u> without anybody realising it's untrue.

<u>Spam e-mail</u> (see page 54) is a major problem. It's possible for spammers to send <u>millions</u> and <u>millions</u> of e-mails to people without even breaking a sweat — great for them, <u>not so great</u> for everyone else.

<u>Plagiarism</u> is when someone tries to pass off <u>another person's work</u> as their own. It's an issue that's magnified by the Internet — because there's <u>so much</u> information available on the Web, many people think they can copy some of it and it'll go <u>unnoticed</u>.

It's Not OK to be Nasty to People

1) Some people feel that the online world is <u>separate</u> from the rest of society. This is not true.

2) For example, people use different methods of <u>online communication</u> to <u>upset</u> other people — '<u>cyber bullying</u>' is a real problem and the consequences are just as <u>awful</u> as normal bullying.

3) <u>Defamation</u> is another problem — some people <u>make up</u> things about other people on websites and blogs because 'it's only the Internet'. But if you get <u>caught</u>, you could be in <u>big trouble</u>.

Staying Safe Online just needs a Little Bit of Common Sense

You're probably more than aware of all the <u>horrid stuff</u> that goes on over the Internet. That's not a reason to stop using it — you just have to <u>use your head</u> to avoid getting in trouble:

When you're communicating with someone over the Internet you should <u>never</u> give anyone your <u>personal details</u> — especially your <u>full name</u>, <u>address</u> or <u>bank details</u>. Don't even give this info over the Internet to people you know — it could be someone pretending to be them, or there could be someone 'listening in', intercepting everything.

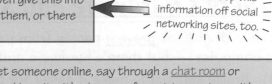

It's best to keep this information off social networking sites, too.

If you get a <u>dodgy-looking email</u> from someone you don't know, <u>delete</u> it — <u>don't</u> open it, or forward it on to other people. If you've accidentally opened the email, <u>don't open any files</u> attached to it. The same thing goes for any <u>hyperlinks</u> — they might look <u>legitimate</u> but they could be very dodgy.

If you've met someone online, say through a <u>chat room</u> or <u>social networking site</u>, it's <u>always</u> safer <u>not</u> to meet up with them in real life. It's unbelievably easy for someone to <u>lie</u> about themselves over the Internet, so you can <u>never</u> be sure that you're being told the <u>whole story</u>...

A lot of <u>pornographic websites</u> are breeding grounds for <u>viruses</u> and other unpleasant computer programs. The best advice is to <u>steer clear of them</u> — if you do somehow end up on one, <u>never</u>, <u>ever download</u> or <u>install</u> any programs that the website asks you to.

When you're using a <u>webcam</u>, don't assume that it's just you and them — there could be <u>people watching</u> you that you <u>can't see</u>. It's also pretty easy to <u>record</u> a webcam feed, so anything <u>silly</u> that you do might come back to <u>haunt you</u>.

Use your noggin before you log in — what a cool rhyme...

... or not. Once you know all of this stuff, <u>tidy</u> your room and bring your <u>washing</u> down. Oh no, I'm still your mum — hold on, I'll change back. You might want to look away... it won't be pretty...

Inequality and Disability

You need to know about the social implications of ICT too.

Different Levels of Access to ICT Affects Individuals...

1) Not everyone has access to a computer and the Internet, or knows how to use them. This creates the potential for a <u>two-tier society</u> — those who are <u>computer-literate</u> (and "information rich"), and those <u>without</u> easy access to computers and the Internet ("information poor").

2) Even now, people <u>without</u> computer skills can find it <u>harder</u> to get a job because a lot of employers have basic computer literacy as a <u>minimum requirement</u> for new staff.

3) And if you're not connected to the <u>Internet</u>, you can <u>miss out</u> on a lot of stuff, for example:

| <u>Online deals</u>, e.g. cheaper car insurance and money-off vouchers. | <u>Educational resources</u>, e.g. revision websites and online encyclopedias. | <u>Cultural things</u>, e.g. new music, funny videos and world news. |

...as well as Cultures and Communities

1) There are loads of <u>different languages</u> used around the world, but most of the stuff on the Web is written in just a <u>few</u> of them — this creates a <u>culture inequality</u>, where people <u>can't access information</u> because it's not in their language.

2) However, because the Web reaches across the world, it's now <u>easier</u> than ever to <u>explore</u> different cultures — all from the <u>comfort</u> of your own home.

3) The Internet can allow people living in countries where contact with the <u>outside world</u> is controlled by the government to get their opinions heard.

4) Some countries <u>don't like</u> the fact that the Internet lets people get any information they want — so they attempt to <u>censor</u> some of it.

- The most famous example of this is in <u>China</u>. The <u>Golden Shield Project</u>, or 'Great Firewall of China', <u>filters out websites</u> that the Chinese government doesn't want people to see.
- This includes websites about <u>foreign news</u>, <u>blogging</u>, and <u>violent</u> or <u>pornographic</u> websites.
- It's a <u>huge project</u> but it <u>angers</u> a lot of people, not just in China, as it <u>prevents</u> people from accessing the information they want to — something which we take for <u>granted</u>.

There's Hardware and Software for People with Disabilities

Some disabilities <u>prevent</u> people from using the usual <u>mouse</u> and <u>keyboard</u> to operate a computer — but there's hardware and software that can <u>overcome</u> this issue:

1) <u>Braille keyboards</u> make it easier for blind computer users to type.

2) <u>Microphones</u> can be used to operate a computer — <u>voice-recognition software</u> is needed to convert the sound into <u>commands</u>. It's useful for things like <u>word processing</u>.

3) Some software converts <u>text to a voice</u>. So if a person can't read, the computer will read it to them.

4) Some operating systems let you <u>customise your desktop</u> to make it <u>easier</u> to use. For example, <u>increasing</u> the <u>text</u> and <u>icon size</u>, and increasing the <u>contrast</u> so things <u>stand out</u> more.

A literate computer — one that reads stuff back to you...

It's quite easy to <u>assume</u> that everyone knows how to use a computer, especially in this 'digital age'. But you need to know that <u>ICT inequality exists</u> and the <u>effects</u> it's having on people.

Political and Environmental Issues

Recording, processing and storing vast amounts of data certainly has <u>benefits</u>.
But there are potential <u>ethical</u> problems too. Have a read of all this...

Technology can Help Protect the Environment

1) <u>Data logging</u> techniques (page 44) can help monitor the <u>environment</u> — for example:
   - <u>concentrations</u> of various <u>gases</u> in the atmosphere (e.g. carbon dioxide),
   - <u>temperatures</u> in different regions and oceans (e.g. using sensors on satellites),
   - <u>loads</u> of other things (e.g. rainfall, soil water content, snow depth, cloud cover...).

2) The hope is that this data can be used to <u>understand</u> atmospheric processes better,
   which should make it easier to decide the best way to deal with <u>climate change</u>.

Technology Brings Political and Ethical Dilemmas

1) Laptops, CDs, memory sticks and hard drives can store <u>lots of data</u> and are <u>extremely portable</u>.
   This is great... until the laptop or the memory stick gets accidentally <u>left</u> somewhere or <u>lost</u> in
   the post. It's happened a few times in recent years, sometimes with very <u>sensitive</u> data.

2) <u>Identity theft</u> has become more common over the years too, and in some ways is
   made easier by advances in technology (e.g. <u>phishing</u> scams — page 77).

3) Britain now has loads of <u>CCTV</u> (closed circuit TV) cameras. They
   make many people <u>feel safer</u>, the police can sometimes <u>identify</u>
   crime suspects from the footage, and they're <u>claimed</u> to <u>deter crime</u>.
   However, some people raise fears of a <u>Big Brother</u> style
   "<u>surveillance society</u>", where your every move is monitored and
   recorded. It's also <u>not clear</u> whether cameras really do deter crime.

4) <u>National government databases</u>, containing details of <u>everyone</u> in a country's population,
   are also controversial. In theory, it's even possible to record and store everyone's <u>DNA profile</u>.

   Supporters claim <u>crimes</u> would be easier to solve, and there'd be less <u>identity theft</u>, for example.
   Others feel governments would have access to private data about citizens that they <u>don't really
   need</u>. Such databases are also <u>expensive</u>, and there's also the risk of <u>data loss</u>.

Technology Can Monitor All Sorts of Everyday Activities

1) Technology can be used to encourage <u>recycling</u> — e.g. "<u>Pay-as-You-Throw</u>" schemes.

2) Microchips (RFID tags, see page 72) are attached to people's <u>wheelie bins</u>.
   These can identify which <u>house</u> each bin belongs to.

3) When the bins are emptied, each bin is <u>weighed</u> by a set of scales built into the bin lorry.

4) People who throw away <u>lots</u> of rubbish would then be charged more for their rubbish to be
   collected. The idea is that those people probably <u>aren't recycling</u> as much as they could.
   Having to <u>pay</u> to throw away <u>recyclable</u> rubbish might make them consider actually <u>recycling</u> it.

5) But this approach <u>isn't</u> popular with everyone.
   - Some people dislike the <u>intrusion</u> — they feel it's like having
     "spies in their bins", keeping an eye on what they throw away.
   - Others feel it's just an excuse to bring in another <u>tax</u>.

For your recycling bins only — a spy film to look forward to...

So there you go... it all gets a bit <u>complicated</u>, even when you're not expecting it. But you still
need to know it all. So <u>learn</u> the stuff, and then <u>test</u> how much you know. <u>I'll be watching</u>.

Revision Summary for Section Ten

Fantastic — you've reached the end of the book... Only joking. You're not going anywhere until you've done this last lot of questions. If you're not sure about an answer, look it up, then try the question again. This section's all about getting you to think about the overall impact of computers, so some of these questions won't have a right or wrong answer, just a good or bad one.

1) What data is covered by the Data Protection Act?
2) Explain the eight principles covered in the Act (yes — all of them).
3) What is the Personal Data Guardianship Code designed for?
4) Describe the five principles of the Code (don't pretend you're not enjoying this).
5) What three things are illegal under the Computer Misuse Act?
6) Explain three measures that can be taken to reduce the risk of damage to hardware.
7) How does intrusion detection help to protect networks?
8) What is phishing?
9) Describe one procedure that banks use to protect your data online.
10) Identify two health problems from the overuse of computers, and explain their causes.
11) Explain three ways that the risks associated with computer use can be reduced.
12) Explain three things that are covered by the Health and Safety (Display Screen Equipment) Regulations 1992.
13) What sorts of jobs have computers replaced humans in performing?
    Give two examples of such jobs.
14) Name three industries that have been created by the increased use of computers.
15) Describe how ICT can be used to automatically control stock levels.
16) Explain the effect of improvements in ICT on the location of businesses.
17) Describe two emerging technologies that may affect businesses and other organisations in the future.
18) What is teleworking? Describe one advantage and one disadvantage of teleworking.
19) How have improvements in ICT increased some people's job satisfaction?
20) Describe what collaborative working is.
21) Explain how a group plan and project management helps collaborative working.
22) Describe two situations where collaborative working might be used.
23) Describe three pieces of software that make collaborative work easier.
24) Explain what teleconferencing is. Describe one advantage and one disadvantage of teleconferencing.
25) Name two things that need to be controlled for effective file management.
26) Describe two ways of securing data while it's being transferred.
27) In your own words, describe what's meant by: a) spam, b) plagiarism.
28) Describe four ways of increasing online safety.
29) Give two effects of the inequality in access to ICT on people.
30) Describe two things that can help disabled people to use computers.
31) Describe one way that technology can help to protect the environment.
32) Explain one political and one ethical problem that technology has caused.
33) Describe how technology can be used to encourage recycling.

Index

Index

Index

Index